DEEP RED

DEEP RED VOLUME 4, NUMBER 1

CONTENTS

Front Cover: "Putrid" Matt Carr
Back Cover photo: Scott Gabbey
TOC Illustration: Stephen R. Bissette

PUBLISHER

Tom Skulan

EDITOR-IN-CHIEF

John Szpunar

MANAGING & COPY EDITOR

Kaz Sánchez

ART DIRECTOR

James Whiting

CONTRIBUTING WRITERS

Stephen R. Bissette

Chris Poggiali

Graham Rae

Kris Gilpin

Greg Goodsell

Dennis Daniel

Shane M. Dallmann

Nick Cato

Mike Hunchback

Bruce Holecheck

David Zuzelo

Art Ettinger

John Szpunar

GRAPHIC ARTISTS

Matt Carr

Eric Rot

Stephen R. Bissette

Chas. Balun

STAFF PHOTOGRAPHERS

Greg Goodsell

Tom Skulan

FOUNDING EDITORS

Chas Balun & Chris Amouroux

Weng's Chop and Monster! editor Tim Paxton, Deep Red staffer David Zuzelo, comic book artist Neil Vokes, Brian Zuzelo, editor John Szpunar, Deep Red staffers Kris Gilpin and Chris Poggiali, and journalist Michael Gingold break bread at FantaCon 2013. Blood brothers, all!

THE CREDITS...

FANTACO ENTERPRISES

We dedicate this issue of Deep Red to its founder, the late Chas Balun—a man who touched more lives than he would have ever dreamed possible...

For Pat Petric

THANK YOU: Stephen R. Bissette, Dennis Daniel, Graham Rae, Kris Gilpin, Greg Goodsell, Shane M. Dallmann, Chris Poggiali, Nick "The Yak" Cato, Mike Hunchback, Bruce Holecheck, David Zuzelo, Art Ettinger, Matt Carr, Eric Rot, James Whiting, Michael J. Weldon, Del Howison, Donald Farmer, Mike Howlett, Lon Kerr, Jamie Chimino, Mitch Davis, Tony Timpone, Stephen Biro, Suzie Ayala, Jeff Cleveringa, David Edward Szpunar, Jimmy McDonough, Mike McPadden, Scot R. Miller, Shawn Lewis, and Mike Raso

In memory of Rick Sullivan and Dallas Mayr

EDITORIAL

Let's set the stage, kids. Let's get this party started right. Let's dim the lights and crack open the window so we can hear the evening breeze whistle through the room. It puts a chill in the air, and that's just what the doctor ordered. Hell—forget the lights. Turn 'em off. There's a moon out tonight, and the ghostly glow that it casts is PERFECT for some late-night reading.

Not convinced? Give it a try. Things like this ALWAYS work best when you follow the doctor's orders, and besides— you're under OUR spell now.

Are you all settled in? Good. Allow me to introduce you to the latest issue of Deep Red.

"What the hell?" you ask. "Deep Red is back?"

Yes, it is—and with a VENGEANCE, at that.

How did we get here? Where are we going? Who's at the wheel? That, my friends, is what editorials are for.

To briefly introduce myself, my name is John Szpunar. Years ago, I was the head of Barrel Entertainment, a DVD company that released films such as Jörg Buttgereit's Nekromantik, Roger Watkins' Last House on Dead End Street, and Harry Kümel's Malpertuis. I am the author of the upcoming Blood Sucking Freak! The Life and Films of the Incredible Joel M. Reed and the bestselling Xerox Ferox: The Wild World of the Horror Film Fanzine—a book that would have never existed, if not for the inspiration of Chas and his work.

Around a year ago, FantaCo's Tom Skulan asked me if I might be interested in reviving Chas Balun's Deep Red as the

editor-in-chief. I was flattered, to say the least, but I was apprehensive. Could I EVER do such an influential magazine justice? Could I possibly get the core staff of Chas' groundbreaking mag to come on board? Did I have it in me to follow in the big man's footsteps? Only one way to find out. I took a deep breath and said, "Yes." With that simple answer, my journey began.

Like everyone reading these pages, I have been obsessed with horror movies for as long as I can remember. I was also a big fan of monster mags and horror film fanzines. I read as many as I could get my hands on. The Splatter Times. Sleazoid Express. Fangoria. The Gore Gazette. Sleazy little things like Subhuman. I could go on and on, but the simple fact is this: Chas Balun's Deep Red was THE major player in those days. The be-all and end-all. To call me obsessed with the magazine would only scratch the surface of my mania.

Deep Red was the magazine that had it all. Chas could always deliver a sharp, intelligent, and hilarious volley of words, and they ALWAYS hit their target. No fools were suffered gladly! If Chas called your film out as a monster dog, that was the END of the story. In fact, thanks to the big man himself, I have never seen Return of the Living Dead, Part II, Ghoulies, or (wait for it!) Monster Dog. Criminal activity, I'm sure, but it was good to be informed.

So here we are, fiends! Deep Red has risen from the grave... with the original core of contributors leading the charge! That's right! Steve Bissette, Dennis Daniel, Greg Goodsell, Shane M. Dallmann, Kris Gilpin, and Graham Rae are together again, for the first time in over 28 years! And that's not all! Acclaimed genre artists and journalists Matt Carr, Eric Rot, Chris Poggiali, Nick

Graham Rae, Stephen R. Bissette, Dennis Daniel, John Szpunar, and Kris Gilpin at FantaCon 2013.

Photo by Lynda Daniel

Cato, David Zuzelo, Art Ettinger, Bruce Holecheck, and Mike Hunchback have joined the team—a team that will undoubtedly continue to grow and (in the words of Dennis Daniel) influence a new generation! Needless to say, we are all VERY excited about things. You won't believe what we have planned! With that said, here is our battle cry…

It is our intent to be true to the integrity and legacy of Chas Balun's groundbreaking magazine. At the same time, we fully realize that times have changed. Sadly, Chas is no longer with us. That does not mean that the magazine should not continue.

We will continue where Chas left off. Nobody knows more than we do what big shoes we have to fill. Still—we are confident that we can do it.

Deep Red will continue to surprise. One of the things that made Deep Red so special (and different from the other magazines that once flooded the marketplace) was its broad range and scope. Deep Red celebrated things that no other magazine dared to touch, yet alone acknowledge. In the age of the internet, Deep Red will continue to deliver news, reviews, interviews, and information that you will find nowhere else. That's a promise.

Deep Red will continue to inspire. One of the best things about reading Chas' work was the feeling of brotherhood that ALWAYS seeped through. He always encouraged young writers, filmmakers, FX artists, and illustrators to believe in their dreams. These sentiments inspired a new generation of horror fans, your editor included. The baton must be passed. The baton WILL be passed.

Honesty is the ONLY policy. The greatest thing about Chas and his writing was his honesty. He told things as they were, without fear or regret. We will continue in this tradition, and will NEVER be afraid to criticize. Monster dogs will always be treated as such. We are not afraid to tell the truth. After all… that's why we're here. ["Except, of course, I had some good things to say about Monster Dog!"— Shane M. Dallmann] See what I mean?

Books are important. We firmly believe that nothing will EVER take the place of the printed page. Words printed on real paper are important, and they will ultimately survive. Electronic information has a way of disappearing without warning. Books and magazines do not. Our goal is to remind our readers that printed information is vital and timeless.

Let's have some FUN! With all of that said, let's get down to the meat of things. Deep Red has always been about family. It has always been about the wonderful feelings that we ALL encounter whenever we sit down in front of a comic book, TV set, or movie screen. It has always been about the monsters and things that go bump in the night—be they new or old—that we encounter, embrace, and fall in love with. Let's make the most of it and paint this town RED!

John Szpunar, editor-in-chief

HERE'S BLOOD IN YOUR EYE

Back from the Dead

Dennis Daniel

OK, so where were we…

Oh, yeah! We were here almost 30 years ago and then… we weren't anymore. "We" being me.

But… we're baaaaaaaaaaaaaack! (Couldn't resist.)

A lot of bloody water has oozed under the bridge since last we spoke, my Deep Red brethren and sistren. I'll be celebrating my 58th birthday this year, and I'm thrilled to say that my love for horror has not diminished an iota! There have been some truly amazing horror films—way, way, way too numerous to mention at the moment. When our new editor John Szpunar asked me for a column, I decided to talk about some recent stuff. We can delve deeper on other films in further issues. A 30-year gap is a lot to cover!

The question I am asked, to this day, by those that know I love horror is, "What scares you?"

I mean, isn't that what this is all about? Being scared? But, of course, it is virtually impossible to scare us tried and true chunkblowers. I mean, what's gonna knock our dicks in the dirt? We've seen it all, right?

Truth is, I don't get scared anymore. But I can still enjoy trying!!!

Photo design by John Twomey

Before I list the titles, I want to mention briefly the joys of real on set special make-up effects instead of CGI. I know CGI has its place, but it basically sucks in horror films. Those of you my age and from my generation will remember that we lived for these films not only for the stories, but for the gore effects… done live, right there, on camera, by super clever and talented motherfuckers like Tom Savini, Bruce Spaulding Fuller, Everett Burrell, the late, great John Vulich, Rob Bottin, Rick Baker, Greg Nicotero, and Kevin Yagher. We loved the FX because we knew they were literally CREATED BY HAND! I think some of the reasons why I enjoy these films so much is they did it the old-fashioned way in many cases, and it made a big difference.

So, here's some recent films since the last issue of Deep Red that I truly love.

First and foremost is Rob Zombie's The Devil's Rejects (2005). To me, this is a PERFECT horror film and homage to '70s style filmmaking. Right down to the grain of the film, it is just a joy from beginning to end. And what a soundtrack! Zombie used rock music that fits the story in every way. I can never listen to "Free Bird" again without thinking of the ending. This film is twisted. It's fucked up! It's filled to the brim with great character actors from classic horror and '70s films… like Sid Haig and Ken Foree. It's funny, too! It's a film made with love by a man very much our blood brother, who adores this stuff so much that he has to make

also adore his House of 1000 Corpses (2003). These are two films my wife Lynda and I watch ALL THE TIME! They never grow old on us. I wish there were other filmmakers out there who could do films like this.

I actually liked the remake of Evil Dead (2013). I thought the drug angel made it very interesting and different. It's very DARK, too. No humor at all, really. The story update worked for me. A drug addict who is going though withdrawal (and has enough shit to deal with) gets possessed by the evil dead? Great fucking idea! A very cool directorial debut by Fede Alvarez.

Fuck all those other remakes!!! All those truly shitty Texas Chain Saw Massacre, Nightmare of Elm Street, Last House on the Left (et cetera, et cetera) remakes and re-imaginings and 3D versions and whatever the fuck! Night of the Living Dead in 3D? Eat me!

There are two clown horror films I've really enjoyed on Netflix. The first is Stiches (2012), a truly bizarre and gory clown film that has some of the funniest, most inventive REAL gore effects I've seen in quite a while. It's a horror comedy, and it worked for me. The second, Clown (2014), was just an awesome story about a clown suit that doesn't come off, possesses your very soul, and turns you into a fucking clown demon.

I fucking loved The Babdook (2014). Original. Scary (yes… this one has some cool scares) and a very interesting monster. Well written and acted. Very, very original, too. The kid in the film can get on your nerves, but for the most part, it's awesome.

I'm tight for time this issue folks, so let me close by saying that there was one CGI film I actually enjoyed… the prequel to The Thing (2011). It had the same vibe as John Carpenter's, and really did a fabulous job of meshing the two films together. Most of the FX were CGI, although they did have some on camera stuff, but I felt it worked and was needed… especially when the two bodies meld into one and give us a creature we remember, in its destroyed and burned form, from the original. Great acting too… which always helps.

So that's it for now my blood-dripped lovelies. Next issue we'll get more in-depth. By then, hopefully, the remake of Suspiria will be out there for us to ponder. Romero's son is also trying to make a prequel to NOTLD. We'll see…

Oh, just one more thing… FUCK SUPER HERO MOVIES! Too many! Although I did LOVE Dr. Strange (2017) and, of course, The Dark Knight (2008)… which, in many ways, is a horror film thanks to the astonishing Oscar winning performance of Heath Ledger as the Joker.

Keep it RED.

MASTER OF MOTION PICTURE MARKETING!

Deep Red Talks with Exploitation Promoter/Distributor Lon Kerr

by Chris Poggiali

otice: Due to the
nusual subject
natter and explicit
resentation of this
notion picture, onl
mature adults shou
attend.

"THE DEAD SHALL RISE
AND WALK THE EARTH"

THE GATES OF HELL

JERRY ZIMMERMAN/MICHAEL FRANZESE PRESENT
"THE GATES OF HELL"
Starring CHRISTOPHER GEORGE • KATHERINE MACCOLL • ROBERT SAMPSON
Story and Screenplay by LUCIO FULCI & DANNY SACCHETTI
Directed by LUCIO FULCI • Color by MGM LABORATORIES
An MPM Release © 1983

THIS FILM CONTAINS SCENES WHICH
MAY BE CONSIDERED SHOCKING. NO
ONE UNDER 17 WILL BE ADMITTED.

If you lived near a drive-in during the first half of the 1980s, chances are damn near 100% that at least one memorably trashy double or triple feature from Motion Picture Marketing arrived in your town and spent a steamy summer weekend cleaning up at the box-office. A ubiquitous presence on the drive-in circuit between 1979 and 1985, MPM specialized in retitled reissues of everything from The Corpse Grinders and Invasion of the Bee Girls to Switchblade Sisters and Eaten Alive before finding its greatest success with Lucio Fulci's The Gates of Hell. The company was founded in September 1978 by John L. Chambliss (president and general sales manager), Lon Kerr (vice president of marketing), and Mike Mahern (vice president of advertising and publicity), all three of whom had recently resigned from their executive positions at EMC Film Corp., a distribution outfit headed by exploitation king M.A. Ripps of Poor White Trash infamy. Prior to his tenure with Ripps, Kerr worked for 20th Century Fox, the well-known film marketing agency Jack Wodell Associates, and such DIY film folks as Bruce Brown, Raphael Nussbaum, and Tom Laughlin— all valuable experiences that prepared him for the down 'n' dirty world of drive-in distribution. "It was like the wild west," Kerr says with a laugh. "We all fought like cats and dogs for screen time. It was 'anything goes' to get screen time." Although the major studios were beginning to muscle out the independents with saturation bookings of big budget blockbusters, MPM managed to hit pay dirt right out of the gate with Cemetery Girls and Grave Desires, a horror double bill that instantly established their breezy, sleazy formula for success: a suggestive title and rhyming tag line, a black-and-white photo of three scantily-clad models on a barely-dressed set, and no billing block on the posters or ads to help moviegoers identify the actual movie behind the tantalizing tableau (in this case it was Dracula's Great Love and The Vampire's Night Orgy, a double bill of English-dubbed Spanish horror movies that had been in circulation for five years, with the former already playing on late-night TV). Films that barely earned flat-rate booking fees a year earlier were suddenly in demand thanks to the company's attention-grabbing ads. In fact, MPM's campaigns were so successful that they were copied by more established companies like Independent-International

(Cathouse Cowgirls), Saturn International (High School Teasers), and New Line Cinema (Good Time Girls). During its six-year lifespan, MPM released nearly 30 movies, resulting in over $40 million in theatrical sales, before the company imploded near the end of 1984. For your education and enjoyment, Deep Red is proud to present this exclusive interview with Lon Kerr, master of motion picture marketing!

DEEP RED: When The Gates of Hell came out, it was the talk of my school.

"THE DEAD SHALL RISE AND WALK THE EARTH"

TWILIGHT OF THE DEAD

JERRY ZIMMERMAN MICHAEL FRANZESE PRESENT "TWILIGHT OF THE DEAD" Starring CHRISTOPHER GEORGE • KATHERINE MACCOLL • ROBERT SAMPSON • Story and Screenplay by LUCIO FULCI & DANNY SACCHETTI • Directed by LUCIO FULCI • Color by MPM LABORATORIES • THIS FILM CONTAINS SCENES WHICH MAY BE CONSIDERED SHOCKING. NO ONE UNDER 17 WILL BE ADMITTED. • An MPM Release © 1985

STARTS FRIDAY
AT A THEATRE OR DRIVE-IN NEAR YOU

"That was part of our ad gimmick! Don't go see this! You cannot go see this! It's too intense!"

Kids were daring each other to see it.

LON KERR: [Bursts into laughter] Oh man! Just last week, I was tellin' a buddy of mine about Gates of Hell. "You gotta see it," I said. "There's a great part where a drill bit goes through a guy's head and comes out the other side!" He said, "You're sick, dude!" "Nah, man—it's great!" And that made the cover of Fangoria! I've still got that issue someplace. Or how about when that gal turns inside out? When I first saw that, I needed a six-pack of beer just to get through the scene!

RED: There was a reason for that warning, "This film contains scenes which may be considered shocking…"

LK: That was part of our ad gimmick! Don't go see this! You cannot go see this! It's too intense! We stuck that little box on every movie, and y'know what? The more we told them not to go see the movies, the more they went!

RED: My local drive-ins got almost all of the MPM releases.

LK: You were in Syracuse, right? That was Ike Erlichman's territory, Frontier Amusements. At one point, I knew all the sub-distributors, every city in the country, all their theaters and drive-ins, I knew their TV stations, knew how much the TV spots cost, how much the newspaper ads cost… We had a formula at MPM, and we almost couldn't lose. We had a mathematician show us how to do it. Let's say we wanted to open in 12 or 13 theaters in Upstate New York. I could pick some little theater, pick the Wednesday night gross, and extrapolate the entire week's gross from one theater. I could tell you almost how much all the other theaters would do, within a couple hundred dollars. So we could predict what we were going to make, and from that I could figure out how much I could spend on advertising.

RED: It sounds like you learned the business from people like M.A. Ripps before you co-founded MPM in 1978.

LK: Mike Ripps was a master of exploitation and I learned much from him that enabled me to become successful in marketing exploitation movies, but I gained my expertise on the United States while working for Yamaha, which is also how I got into the film business. When the Japanese motorcycle manufacturers first came over here, they had a hard time getting people to buy their products. Up to that point it had always been Harleys, right? So, I was working for an ad agency, and we came up with this clever idea to teach people how to ride motorcycles. My job was to fly to a market, meet with the dealerships, and put together programs to teach people how to ride. The biggest one I did was in New York, where I had over 15,000 people in Nassau Coliseum. It was great, but for about a year and a half I didn't have a home. I lived on a jet.

RED: You mean you did a lot of traveling?

LK: I mean my home was the jet! When I went in for the interview, they said, "You won't really need a car." I said, "Oh? How much travel is involved?" They said, "Wellllll, you won't need a car. [Clears his throat] By the way, you won't need a house or an apartment either." "How much travel is involved?!" [Laughs] I didn't see L.A. for more than a year! But I got to see pretty much every other city in the country. So, I was doing that, and one day the Japanese pulled me in and said that they wanted me to manage their new promotion, Yamaha Presents: On any Sunday. Bruce Brown and Steve McQueen were re-releasing their motorcycle documentary On Any Sunday, and Yamaha was fronting the money. I said, "I like what I'm doing. I don't want to work in the film business." Well, the Japanese don't take no for an answer. They were putting large sums of money into the new promotion, and they wanted me to oversee their cash. They literally told me I was the only guy they trusted! So, that's how I got into the film business. I was forced into it.

RED: Did you meet with Steve McQueen?

LK: No, but I got a call from him one day. He said, "How's business?" Boy did that crack me up! In those days, he was a superstar, and for him to call me and ask, "How's business?" "Well, Steve, we did this-and-this-and-this in one theater, that-and-that-and-that in another theater..." [Laughs] That's the only time I ever talked to him. Apparently, he was going through a divorce with Ali McGraw at the time, and she didn't know about this one partnership he had.

RED: When did you work for 20th Century Fox?

LK: I went to them sometime in '75 as an advertising and publicity manager. I was very excited about joining a major studio, but it turned out the big slogan there was "26 for '76"—26 losers in a row: Whiffs, Lucky Lady, Royal Flash, Take a Hard Ride... what else? Sherlock Holmes'

"THE DEAD SHALL RISE"

REVENGE OF THE DEAD

MOTION PICTURE MARKETING
PRESENTS
"REVENGE OF THE DEAD"
Starring JOHN STACY • ANN CANOVAS • GABRIEL LAVIA
A Film By PUPI AVATI • Director of Photography FRANK COLLI

THIS FILM CONTAINS SCENES WHICH MAY BE CONSIDERED SHOCKING. NO ONE UNDER 17 WILL BE ADMITTED.

Prints by
GETTY FILM LABORATORIES
AN MPM RELEASE © 1984

"The worst decision was Savage Streets, which caused a lot of problems and was the single reason why our company went under."

Smarter Brother—all these movies that just died—Mother, Jugs & Speed...

RED: Some of those are really good movies!

LK: A couple of them are great! Next Stop, Greenwich Village—outside of New York, that died. The Rocky Horror Picture Show is a cult classic now, but at the time, it was just another loser, plus it didn't help that the sales people weren't selling it. They weren't even mentioning it to the buyers. They were like "I'm not gonna sell some faggot movie!" Alan Ladd, Jr., who was [head of creative affairs] at Fox at the time, got word that the publicity and advertising people actually liked Rocky Hor-

ror, so he called us into his office for a secret meeting at midnight on a Friday night. He did that so the sales people wouldn't know. The only people invited were the publicity and advertising people, because we were all younger than the sales staff, and we thought the show was great. Keep in mind, nobody saw Alan Ladd, Jr.! He was like a god in those days! [Laughs] So, he called us in and said, "Listen, we're a million and a half dollars into this show and we're going to lose the million and a half, so this is what I want you to do: create a buzz that will force the sales people to sell this movie." He was enlisting us as his personal guys to go out and sell the movie, and that's what we did. I actually had the first date in the country for Rocky Horror. It was a disaster.

RED: Where was that?

LK: A theater called the University Flick, right across the street from Ohio State in Columbus. There were 30,000 students roughly in those days—we figured we couldn't go wrong with that many young people, right? So I went to Columbus to promote the thing, did newspaper and TV interviews, placed the ads, put up flyers. This was the original campaign, with the guys in the garter belts. The next thing I know, all these young drunk guys are coming in and throwing beer bottles at the screen. I was in there to check audience response. "Hey! You've got something to do with this movie?" I was the only guy there in a suit! They started throwing stuff at me and shouting, "Faggot!" It was a little on the life-threatening side! I'm talkin' drunk frat guys, y'know? That's when I called the studio and said, "We better get rid of all the garter belt stuff and just go with the lips that are at the opening of the movie."

RED: "A different set of jaws."

LK: They changed the campaign overnight. I never got any credit for it, but the "lips" campaign changed the way the movie was perceived. The truth is, at Fox I got really good at selling marginal movies. That's where I learned to look for the angles.

RED: What's another example of looking for angles?

LK: Well, one of my jobs was to take the stars on tour, so for Take a Hard Ride, I was with Jim Kelly in Detroit, which was a big market for black titles in those days. I was in the Hotel Pontchartrain lobby, and all of a sudden, I noticed all these gorgeous black people—men dressed in tuxes, women in party dresses. I'm like, wow, something's going on here, right? So I went in there. Keep in mind, I didn't know where I was going, I just sensed something was up. It turned out some guy who was top of the top of the social loop in Detroit was throwing a party and had like 1,500 people there dressed to the hilt, and they were all black. I'm like, "Ain't this a trip?" So, I found the guy throwing the party and I said, "Hey listen, I got an interesting situation. I work for 20th Century Fox, and I've got an actor in town. Do you mind if he comes to your party?" The guy said, "What's his name?" "Jim Kelly." "Oh yeah, I know Jim Kelly! Sure!" So Jim came in, and the guy brought him up to the podium and introduced him to the whole party. You couldn't ask for a more gracious entrée, and we had a great time. We partied 'til four or five in the morning! You gotta look for opportunities where you can find them. The film did well in Detroit because all these people had met Jim Kelly and the word got out.

RED: After your stint at Fox, you went to Jack Wodell Associates. What kind of work did you do there?

LK: I did the premiere for The Passover Plot, a religious show where Zalman King played Jesus. I orchestrated a demonstration against the movie by church groups for the premiere in Beverly Hills. At the same time, I worked on the very first skateboard movie, Freewheelin'. I had wanted to get a bear to "hang ten" off a skateboard,

but I couldn't find a bear to do it for me, so I had to settle for Bruno, a Rockhopper penguin who was famous at the time for a Ford commercial. Busch Gardens gave us their facility, so that's where we shot the

John   *Lon*   *Mike*

Season's Greetings From MPM

"That was part of our wackiness. We'd get our picture taken with a beautiful model and then sign it, 'Season's greetings from MPM!'"

pictures. I couldn't believe how much penguins poop, man. The guys at Busch Gardens were like, "Hey, you wanted this, you clean it up." We only had one skateboard and I had to keep hosing it down!

RED: You also worked for Tom Laughlin at Billy Jack Enterprises. What was that job interview like?

LK: I went to his mansion in Bel Air or wherever, and his servant—in a little servant uniform—met me at the front door and ushered me out to a chair by a pool.

Tom Laughlin came out in a bathing suit and white robe, sat next to me, and interviewed me by the pool. I thought, "Well, this is different!" I'm sure it was to impress me. Once I got the job, he said, "Take whatever money you need and hire a secretary—and make sure she's beautiful." [Laughs] I hired a little French girl, Paulette. She was a knockout. Gorgeous! On her first day he walked by, took one look at her and gave me a "thumbs up"—All right, Lon!

RED: So, he was easy to work with?

LK: Wellllllllll… [Laughs] At the beginning, yes, but as things started to unravel, he became a problem. He'd made millions and millions four-walling those first couple of movies, but after The Trial of Billy Jack, the show was over and he just didn't get it. The Master Gunfighter died, Train Ride to Hollywood died, and then he overspent on Billy Jack Goes to Washington. He had to have the chairs crafted exactly the same as the actual ones from the Senate. "They've gotta be exactly the same!"

RED: What was your official job title at Billy Jack Enterprises?

LK: I was national public relations/publicity director and Mike Mahern was national advertising manager, and boy did we have our hands full with Billy Jack Goes to Washington. It was really long, like two and a half hours, and it was just him preaching. I took one look at it and thought, "Oh my God, I've gotta sell this thing?" That's why I sent all those people to the premiere in Washington, to try to put some power into it: E.G. Marshall, Pat O'Brien, Lucie Arnaz, Frank Capra, Jr. I even got Walter Cronkite to show up. We got a lot of publicity, but people hated the movie, so it was pretty much downhill from there.

RED: It barely played anywhere after the world premiere in D.C.

LK: Once it died, he started to turn sour and moody. I put up with a lot of stuff and it didn't bother me, but one day I was in the conference room with 12 people, we're sitting around this long mahogany table and he's seated at the end of it. I was supposed to have a writer from the Toronto Star come down and interview his wife. So he looked around the table, and his muscles started to pump out of his neck 'cause he was angry and he yelled, "Lon! Where's the guy who's supposed to interview Dody?!" I said, "I don't know, man. He's caught in traffic?" Well, he just went ballistic, banging on the table and yelling, "My wife is a major star!"—which she wasn't—[Laughs]—sayin' all this bullshit, and then he jumped up and I really thought he was gonna come across the table at me. I knew some martial arts in those days, so I jumped up thinking he was coming at me. I wanted to protect myself. Everybody else was just cowering. It was pretty close to fisticuffs. At that point, I said, "Hey, you can keep the job," and I quit right there. I hated to quit because it was a great deal, but I wouldn't put up with that kind of stuff from anybody.

RED: Tell me about Raphael Nussbaum of Burbank International Pictures.

LK: Raphael was of the generation before me. He was from Germany, and none of the Germans trusted Americans, so they'd give Raphael their movies and he would translate them into English. That was his forté, editing and translating them into English and then taking the movies out into the marketplace. There were a slew of them—Run Virgin Run, Barbed Wire Dolls, 2069: A Sex Odyssey—but my favorite was Journey into the Beyond.

RED: That's a mondo-type paranormal documentary with narration by John Carradine and warning bells that sound before the gruesome scenes to alert the squeamish viewers in the audience to close their eyes.

LK: I handled the release of that, wrote all the press stuff, and did the premiere in

New Orleans. Barehanded surgery, levitation, life after death… When I was looking for something to use in the promotion, I met a satanic priest who said, "Come to one of our services." In those days, I would do anything for publicity. Well, almost

Some things never rest in peace.

Barry Allen Productions Presents "FUNERAL HOME"
Starring KAY HAWTRY and LESLEH DONALDSON Special Guest Star BARRY MORSE
Featuring HARVEY ATKIN Executive Producer BARRY ALLEN Produced and Directed by WILLIAM FRUET
Associate Producer PATRICK DOYLE Written by IDA NELSON Director of Photography MARK IRWIN
Music Composed and Conducted by JERRY FIELDING Editor RALPH BRUNJES C.F.E.
Produced with the participation of the Canadian Film Development Corporation
An MPM Release ©1982

"When I was looking for something to use in the promotion, I met a satanic priest who said, 'Come to one of our services.'"

anything. So I went to this satanic temple in Hollywood. He asked me to sit in front, right next to the podium, and he started reading from the Satanic Bible, while I was like three feet away from him. Then he started talking about how he got his power. Apparently, he had been in a car accident and had been totally paralyzed, but over the course of two years, he would practice

working on one muscle at a time and got to the point where he could move individually almost every muscle in his body. Then he proceeded to take his shirt off and show us—I mean, he was really doing all of this for me—how he could move one muscle at a time, in his back, his front, his abs, this little muscle over here on the left... Well, that was impressive. Then he hooked himself up to a monitor and stopped his heart for a little while, then he restarted it, then he stopped it again. I thought, "Well, that's a little boring, but I guess it's cool." So then he brought out a big razor-sharp sword and set a piece of paper over it to slice it in two and then asked me to touch it to feel how sharp it was. Hmm, I wonder where this is going. [Laughs] He put up two stanchions right in front of me, put the sword across them sharp-side-up, to demonstrate his power and how when he's doing his thing he's not part of reality. He laid right over it in front of me. I saw him, on a razor-sharp sword—which I had just touched—put all of his weight on it, and it went right up to his spinal column. I'm going, "Oh my God, oh my God, this is great!" I was afraid he was going to get cut in half, but he did it! For the big finale, he took some girl, I think his assistant, hypnotized her, put her into a trance, had her lie down on the floor—again, right in front of me—and put a cinderblock on her stomach. Then he picked up a sledgehammer, came running across the room, took one big swing and hit the cinderblock on her stomach, and I mean a full-powered swing straight down which broke the cinderblock. When he snapped her out of the trance, she was totally unharmed. I'm like, "All right! We're talking something big here!" I was all ready to use him on national TV for the premiere of Journey into the Beyond, but then he said, "There's just one little thing." I said, "What's that?" He said, "I have to read from the Satanic Bible." This was going to be on national TV! I said, "Noooo, you're not going to read from the Satanic Bible." He said, "Well, that's where I get my power from." Forget it! Not gonna happen! Can you see me on television having some guy reading from the Satanic Bible? [Laughs]

RED: What did you end up doing for the premiere in New Orleans?

LK: I hung a guy upside down from a crane and set him on fire for the drive-in opening, and he almost lost a leg to gangrene. He assured me that he could do it. I made him do a few stunts for me beforehand, where I watched him escape from a strait jacket, and then I set him on fire to make sure he could do that. The problem was that when he was hanging upside down, some of the fluid went down his leg. It wasn't lighter fluid but some other stuff that would go up fast. He was OK, it was just scary for a while there and I was mad at him for not taking the proper safety precautions.

RED: Mike Ripps' company, EMC Film Corporation, was based in Florida?

LK: Well, Ripps and his partner, Harry Gurwitch, stayed in Miami while John Chambliss and I did all the work and made all the money for them. We hired Mike Mahern, who had worked with me earlier at Jack Wodell. Mike was our brainiac. He was a very sharp guy when it came to numbers. We were the three guys really running EMC. We had a luxury office in Century City with our own 80-seat screening room. Can you imagine the expense of having such a large screening room in Century City? It sure impressed a lot of clients!

RED: I had no idea the EMC releases were that successful.

LK: Naked Rider made tons of money, and Convention Girls and At Last, At Last were also very successful. Those were the three we worked on. There was a lot of money flowing on that gig, but it was all going to Florida and none of it was coming back to pay our vendors. I was getting guys to do hard work—making posters, doing TV ads—and the Miami boys were

scamming them. They were sucking the company dry is what it amounted to. One day, we called them and said, "Hey, our vendors have to get paid. If they're not going to get paid then we're going to walk out." They thought we were bluffing, so we

THEY EAT THE LIVING

NIGHT OF THE ZOMBIES

MOTION PICTURE MARKETING
Presents
"NIGHT OF THE ZOMBIES"
starring FRANK GARFEELD · MARGIT NEWTON · SELAN KARAY
directed by VINCENT DAWN · music by GOLBIN
director of photography JOHN CABRERA

THIS FILM CONTAINS SCENES WHICH MAY BE CONSIDERED SHOCKING. NO ONE UNDER 17 WILL BE ADMITTED.

An MPM Release © 1983

"I hung a guy upside down from a crane and set him on fire for the drive-in opening, and he almost lost a leg to gangrene."

walked out. The next day, Harry had the doors locked, cancelled our credit cards, and froze us out. That's how John, Mike, and I started Motion Picture Marketing. We were three boys out on the street!

RED: MPM only handled re-releases of older movies during its first two years.

LK: Because we had no budget! We were

operating out of my apartment in Marina del Rey. We literally started the company with $500 between the three of us. We did the photo shoot for Cemetery Girls with that, got an advance for $10,000 from a sub-distributor and voilà, we were in business. We had to talk people into giving us their movies by telling them, "We'll make you money." These were old movies that were played out, or they were with guys who just didn't know how to sell them. Then we had to go out and hustle with the media buying service to give us 90 days to make payment. In the early days, it was sweating bullets all the time.

RED: Did you license these films for re-release or buy them outright?

LK: In the early days, we had to make percentage deals, but we found out a lot of these guys were greedy. No matter how much we paid people, they always thought we were ripping them off. They'd start with no money, we'd make them some money, and then they'd suspect we were making more money than we were, so they'd sue us. It was a mental drain, so we just started buying the stuff outright if we could. Look at The Concrete Jungle. We took a film that had a lot of bad vibes, we went out and made money on it, and I think even the producer, who was a friend of ours, started to make noise about "I thought I'd make more money."

RED: The Cemetery Girls w/ Grave Desires combo attracted a lot of attention with its classic tag line, "They rise at night for more than a bite."

LK: If we had known then what we learned a couple of years later, we would've made a ton of money. We only had 25 prints of each, and the sub-distributors kept asking us to buy more prints, but we didn't want to tell them that we didn't have money. They were going to give us some money, but it just wasn't enough. They wanted us to have 80 or 90 prints. It cost $125,000 for a full complement of prints. We didn't want to spend that kind of money on somebody else's title just to give it back to them six years later, but if we had done that we would've made a million dollars because it went through the roof. We didn't have the credit, so we just couldn't do it. We worked those prints to death! Vampire Playgirls was another one. That made over $500,000 profit with very few prints.

RED: I always wondered if there was a connection between EMC and MPM because the ad campaigns looked so similar, especially Convention Girls with the three women posing around the disclaimer box.

LK: Yeah, we just took those ideas with us. Our ad campaigns always had one to three girls. For Roman Polanski's Forbidden Dreams, we had one girl in that. The others had two or three. The knack was picking the girls. There had to be one dark-haired girl, one blonde, and one brunette—something for everyone! That's how I found Apollonia. She was Patty Kotero at the time. She was nobody, and we splattered her face all around the country.

RED: Not only does Apollonia appear in the ad campaigns for Satan's Playthings, Classroom Teasers, and Chaingang Girls, but she's also in a couple of the MPM holiday cards.

LK: That was part of our wackiness. We'd get our picture taken with a beautiful model and then sign it, "Season's greetings from MPM!" and send the pictures to our sub-distributors and main buyers. They used to look forward to getting those Christmas cards. It was great for business! John and I went on rafting trips down the Colorado and Arkansas Rivers with all the major buyers from General Cinema, National Amusements, AMC and other chains. We were the only ones invited who weren't buyers!

RED: I'm going through some of the MPM ad mats now—Sex Education, Centerfold Spread, Playgirl Gang, Locker Room Girls, Eager Beavers, Naked Stewardesses…

LK: We were really good at coming up with a title—usually two words at the most—shooting the ad campaign, and then going out and trying to find a movie to match it. [Laughs] People couldn't believe how we did stuff!

CEMETERY GIRLS

THEY RISE AT NIGHT
FOR MORE THAN A BITE.

Notice: Due to the unusual subject matter and explicit presentation of this motion picture, only mature adults should attend.

R.I.P.

CRAZED WOMEN DESPERATE FOR SATISFACTION.

R RESTRICTED — UNDER 17 REQUIRES ACCOMPANYING PARENT OR ADULT GUARDIAN

AN **MPM** RELEASE

"There had to be one dark-haired girl, one blonde, and one brunette—something for everyone! That's how I found Apollonia."

RED: Graveyard Tramps…

LK: That's the girl with the scythe, right? I used to have to go to the prop houses and pick out the props, find a coffin, and of course I was the guy who interviewed all the girls. For the Eager Beavers poster, that's me lying on the floor! I was on the cement floor for hours, man! My back hurt so bad, I had to have those girls rub my back afterwards. [Laughs]

RED: Are you one of the guys in the Flesh Grinders ad?

LK: Yes! Mike is getting shoved into the meat grinder and I'm chained to the wall like I'm going to be the next one ground up. We shot that in my apartment in Marina del Rey.

RED: MPM pushed the envelope a bit with Senior Snatch.

LK: Chris Condon loaned us that. It was a 3-D movie called Surfer Girls, but nobody wanted to see 3-D at that point so we said, "You got any flat prints? Give it to us!" We changed the title to The Senior Snatch and did well with it, but some places wouldn't run the ads. I'd tell 'em, "Just change it to a 'C' or black it out"—The Senior CATCH—and we always did better in those cities, y'know? I'd be in stitches because they'd always put a big stupid 'C' or draw a black mark through the 'S' and the people in town would be like, "Hey, they're trying to keep something from us! We better go see what this is about!" [Laughs]

RED: Who did the voices for your radio spots?

LK: "Run for your life! They're right behind you!" That was us doing that! We had the sound of breaking wood, and then we'd yell, "Oh my God!" or "Look out!" That was a blast, man. We used to hire talent, but we figured for the real wacky stuff we could just yell, "Run for your life!"

RED: Final Exam was the first MPM production?

LK: Yeah, that was a crazy deal. We hired someone to produce it and three days into it everyone called us from Earl Owensby's studio in North Carolina and said, "We're gonna quit." What!? We flew down there to see if we could calm things down a little bit, and it turned out he had alienated ab-so-lute-ly everybody. The cast, the crew, they all threatened to quit. We had to fire him and still pay him his producer's fee. We ended up taking over the production ourselves. I'd never made a movie in my life! We ended up spending the next six weeks down there. I'd have to get up and do the ad campaigns and help run the company, and then go out and produce the movie during the day. We were putting in 16-hour days. We'd come in, get two hours sleep, then get up at five or six in the morning to watch dailies, then go out and do it all over again. It was the most stressed out I've been in my whole life. Making a movie is like going to war, plus we were running a company.

RED: Was Mausoleum another MPM production?

LK: No, we acquired that. I'll never forget when we opened that in New York, it was one of the few times I argued with my partner over expenses. As I recall, we bought a single full-page ad in a newspaper that set us back $50,000 or more. The ad had a certain prestige factor and it did help us get a good home video deal, but it was a lot of money. New York was always crazy because we'd have to play like 80 theaters to make up for the media coverage. We used to have to spend anywhere from $125,000 to $200,000 when we played New York. That always made my heart stop. New York and L.A.—I'd sweat bullets those weeks. At the same time, we'd also be playing other cities all over the country. Wherever we could get dates, right? So on any given week, I might be spending half a million dollars on advertising. I used to be like a cat on a hot tin roof! I was nervous all the time! Luckily, these movies were so consistent I could tell you almost to the dollar how much I'd make in every city. Maybe I'd be off by a hundred, two hundred dollars, but I could pretty much tell what I would gross in a given night because I'd already have played the movie somewhere else and all the theaters were consistent. The exception was Heartaches with Margot Kidder and Annie Potts. That was our only loser.

RED: I think that's the only MPM release that didn't play near me.

LK: Every movie we had up to that point

had made money. We committed to the producer to spend $500,000 on it, because to us it was a real movie with real stars. It was a good little movie. All of a sudden, we're choking on prints, choking on advertising

Vampire Playgirls

THEY BITE. THEY SQUEEZE. THEY'RE READY TO PLEASE.

R RESTRICTED
UNDER 17 REQUIRES ACCOMPANYING PARENT OR ADULT GUARDIAN

AN **MPM** RELEASE

"We worked those prints to death! Vampire Playgirls was another one. That made over $500,000 profit with very few prints."

expenditures, and getting no return. I went up to Seattle and did a special art house release up there. It died. Then I came up with a great idea: Let's put it up for Academy Award consideration! So, we spent $25,000 or more running trade ads and all that stuff. When we got to where we were being considered for an Academy Award, I got Margot Kidder up on stage at the Academy to speak, and the next thing I know she's with William Shatner and he's saying, "I hear Heartaches is only playing drive-ins!" That wasn't true at all. I mean, it played some

drive-ins, but it mostly played regular theaters. She said, "Oh yeah," and then started badmouthing us! I was sitting there watching this, all tickled after the work I'd done and she ends up badmouthing our company. That was it for me on releasing decent movies! [Laughs] I think we lost $350,000 and were still committed to spend another $150,000 or something like that, but we decided to just give the movie back to the producer if he would let us out of the contract. So, he did.

RED: How did you find the newer foreign movies like Caged Women and Revenge of the Dead? Did you attend the international markets?

LK: Uhhh… no, that would cost money. [Laughs] No, we'd just tell people to send us cassettes or prints or whatever, and we had our favorite screening room we went to all the time to watch movies and have fun. I think we saw every piece of shit ever made. We had to sit through 40 of them for every one we ended up taking. That's how we found The Gates of Hell. We were sitting around on a Friday afternoon having some beers with our girlfriends and wives, all of us watching this movie. John and I hated it. Well, they loved it! John and I were like, "Really? Huh." We started to smell money, y'know? If two women liked this movie, maybe there was something to it! So we decided to buy it.

RED: Is it true that MPM had originally planned to release Ulli Lommel's The Devonsville Terror as The Gates of Hell?

LK: Ulli was close to finishing The Devonsville Terror but was totally tapped out. We bought the rights and gave him $60,000 to finish it. We had him shoot some bravo scenes to make it a better show, and we were there for some of the shoot, like with the snake and all that good stuff. For us, $60,000 was a lot, so wanted to make sure nothing went wrong. In the process of doing that, we were trying to come up with a better title. Ulli liked The Devonsville Terror but we were like, "No one in the world's gonna see a movie with that title," so we came up with The Gates of Hell.

RED: Meanwhile, The Gates of Hell was originally going to be released as Twilight of the Dead?

LK: Here's what happened with that. When we were getting ready to release it as Twilight of the Dead in L.A., we had a Sunday ad appear in the Los Angeles Times. Monday morning, we got a call from George Romero's attorney, who was threatening to sue us because George thought our ad campaign was too similar to his ['Dead' movies]. We were totally freaked because we had all this money riding on a Friday opening and a guy threatening to sue us and get a temporary restraining order. We didn't think he'd get it done in a five-day period, so we thought we'd take a calculated risk. Once it opens, it's too late, right? But he could certainly tie up our funds. We decided to call him back and ask, "Hey, how about if we change the title and the ad campaign?" Not thinking we could ever do that in time, he said "OK." We needed a new title, so I said, "Let's just call it The Gates of Hell." Man, if I thought I had worked hard on Final Exam! [Laughs] We spent the next 48 hours staying up until four in the morning redoing the radio spots, redoing the television spots, hand rushing the radio and TV spots to the radio and TV stations, redoing the newspaper campaign, redoing the poster, reprinting the posters, and having them hand-delivered to the theaters. This was before email, so the copy had to be hand-delivered to everyone. We had newspaper ads running in Ventura, San Diego, Palm Springs—they had deadlines, and they weren't the day before! [Laughs] They're usually days before! By Wednesday, we had new TV and radio spots on the air, we had new posters in the theaters by late Wednesday and early Thursday, and we had all the prints retitled and in the theaters for opening day on Friday. It cost us $40,000 to redo it all. The movie posters alone cost us $7,000. We redid the whole thing in four days. Four days. It's something you can't tell people. They won't believe you.

RED: The Gates of Hell turned out to be a big hit.

LK: It did around $10 million, which was a lot in those days. It played eight weeks in New York. During the first week, it did $40,000 in just one theater. In fact, we were making so much money off that movie that we lost track of The Devonsville Terror a little bit! [Laughs] I think we basically wrote off $60,000 and said to Ulli, "Here, take the movie back." In those days, you could do stuff like that. We had started

"The worst decision was Savage Streets, which caused a lot of problems and was the single reason why our company went under."

doing Brainwaves, but we pulled the plug on that one, also. We got along with Ulli, I just think the stuff he was making didn't quite agree with us, so we gave them back to him.

RED: The title lettering on the Twilight of the Dead campaign was a total copy of the one used for Dawn of the Dead.

LK: Oh yeah, the whole idea was that George Romero was getting ready to make a new movie, Day of the Dead, and was getting a lot of PR and publicity, and we

thought if we could get our zombie movie into the marketplace first, we could use all that press to our advantage. And that's exactly why The Gates of Hell did so well, because everyone kept thinking it was George Romero's new movie. There was all this publicity about a new 'Dead' movie and we were the first ones out there, so everyone just assumed that was it. Then he ran into some kind of production problems and got tied up, so we shoved out Night of the Zombies—another 'Dead' movie—and then we did Revenge of the Dead. We shoved out three zombie movies before he ever got his to the marketplace, and when Day of the Dead finally did open, it died. We had sucked the market dry! [Laughs] He never knew what hit him! We hit him!

RED: When did Mike Mahern leave MPM to become a screenwriter?

LK: In 1982 or so, we bought him out. He was glad to take a hunk of cash and go. He was a senior executive in the Writers Guild for many years and is now completely out of the movie business.

RED: It seems like MPM went into a tailspin shortly after it entered into co-production deals with Billy Fine and Michael Franzese in April of 1983.

LK: If my partner would have just been satisfied with "little movies", we'd probably still be going strong. We made some really great decisions at the time. One of the best was offloading Mausoleum for a $60,000 advance, which seemed like a lot of money for a new thing called VHS. The worst decision was Savage Streets, which caused a lot of problems and was the single reason why our company went under. There were a lot of bad vibes on that show. Too much money was spent. There were many conflicts over content. I was against it from the beginning, because John wanted to have a rape scene in it. "Come on, we don't really need to have a rape scene." "Oh yes, we need a rape scene! We've got to have a hook!" "Well, I don't think rape is a very good hook…" Over my objections, we put in the rape scene. It was just easier to go along rather than get into a fight, but that scene really worked against us. Then he insisted on using a campaign that I thought was too negative and wouldn't work. I fought him on this and even our lawyers got involved. Franzese's boys were supposed to put in a lot of money for productions, but the money never showed, and then John wrote $190,000 worth of bad checks. Suddenly there were guys with no necks showing up threatening to kill us, and I was like, "Noooo, it's him over there! He wrote the bad checks!" That's when things began to sour on my side.

RED: According to an article in Variety on January 30th, 1985, you took legal action against Chambliss for forcing you out of MPM in order to prevent you from obtaining your full share of the company's profits. Your complaint also charged him with refusing to pay you 20% of the profits from Savage Streets as promised in an agreement from May '84, and for misappropriating MPM assets to develop a film called White Slavery.

LK: He took out $65,000. He had his wife in charge of accounting so I wouldn't know. I said, "Hey, man, if you needed money, you should've just asked me!" Then he took out another $70,000 without me knowing about it, and that's when I said, "I think we're at the end, dude." He couldn't slip out $135,000 without problems. I said, "Why couldn't you just come to me? We were partners!" I realized he was getting closer and closer to Franzese, so I took him out one day and told him, "I don't want anything to do with these people." The next thing I know, he's got me locked out, I've got him locked out, there are security guards blocking the entrances to both offices... It was a mess, man. We had offices right at the edge of Marina del Rey, half a block from the ocean. Our neighbors, who had million-dollar condos, were upset because guys with guns were outside our doors 24/7. Finally, my lawyers convinced me to call off my security guards and deal with him through the legal system. I filed a lawsuit, and eventually he just walked away and gave the whole company to me because the bank was on

my side. After that, everybody in the world was looking for him. He moved to Texas to get far away from everybody, which actually worked because Texas in those days was like the end of the earth. That's when he started doing the [Film Concept Group] stuff down there. He wouldn't dare show up back in L.A.

RED: Joe Bob Briggs mentioned your ousting from MPM in an almost poignant way in his review of Revenge of the Dead.

LK: I was dealing with Joe Bob back when he was just a nobody down in Dallas. He used to get mad at me because I wouldn't screen our movies for him. "Come on, man!" he'd say, "I'll write something really gutsy about them!" [Laughs] You can picture him on the phone saying that, right? "Come on! I won't trash them!" I was like, "Of course you will!" "No, no, no!" So I took a chance on him, and he actually helped us out. I worked with him for years.

RED: Following the collapse of MPM, you started First Cinema Ventures, a company that sold films to pay-per-view and hotel in-room services.

LK: I was one of the first guys around to sell to PPV. No one had ever heard of it. The guys renting the office next to mine in Raleigh Studios were Request Television. They were just a start-up company. I used to go in there, "Hey! What's this pay-per-view thing? How does it work?" They'd say, "Well, people call us and they can order a movie." They were struggling, they had no budget. I said, "Why don't you buy some of my titles?" "OK." At first there was no money— I mean no money—but I figured I was getting in on the ground floor, right? So I specialized in pay-per-view for years. I sold just about every movie I had.

RED: What were some of your biggest successes with pay-per-view?

LK: I did extremely well with Sahara Heat on PPV and brought in well over $300,000 on that show. It has the distinction of being aired three times by Viewers Choice and two or three times by Request TV. That film, along with Honey, were among the few ever shown by these systems as Encore Showings, a concept I sold them on doing initially. Both films grossed

millions at Spectradyne back in the day. Spectradyne picked up both under three separate contracts due to their success.

RED: These days, you're the president of Dreamcatcher Entertainment.

LK: Still in the business! I have Lethal Seduction with Chris Mitchum, Julie Strain, and Joe Estevez, The Reluctant Hitman, The Bikini Detectives, some of the Raphael Nussbaum films like 2069: A Sex Odyssey, I Like the Girls Who Do, and Run Virgin Run. Unfortunately, a lab burned down in the valley and I lost several masters that way. Another lab lost 60 or 70 of my masters, or else they just destroyed them and said, "We couldn't reach you." Then, one of my partners stole my masters and fled to China and is selling them over there. To have all your materials disappear, your negatives and one-inch masters—it's a nightmare. It's not like you can replace them.

RED: If you had the last year of MPM to do over again, what do you think you would do differently to keep the business going?

LK: After I got control of the company—and I mean he literally relinquished all rights to me—I would've come up with another movie immediately and released it. The bank probably would've given me some money to do that. The problem was that he had taken out $150,000 in employee taxes. He was supposed to be paying the state, so now the state of California was coming after me for $150,000. I said, "I wasn't even there at the time!" They said, "That doesn't matter. You were partners." He was in Texas and I was here, so they were breathing down my neck. They kept saying, "We don't care. You were partners." It's like a marriage—if the husband does something, they'll go after his spouse in California! They were on me for years, so I finally had to hire a lawyer. The best thing that ever happened to me was that lawsuit I had filed. My lawyer showed them the lawsuit and convinced them I wasn't there and that I had no control [of MPM] at the time. But yeah, if I could do it over again, that's what I'd do—try to find something and release it. You're only as good as your next movie, right?

Thanks to Lon Kerr and Mike Raso.

Fantasia
INTERNATIONAL FILM FESTIVAL
JULY 13 TO
AUGUST 2
2017
MONTREAL
fantasiafestival.com

BACK TO THE BELLY OF THE BEAST!

Staffer Mike Hunchback attended Fantasia's 2017 Film Festival, eyeballed a slew of new films, and talked about Deep Red founder Chas Balun with Fantasia's co-general director Mitch Davis and Fangoria's Tony Timpone, both of whom are co-directors of international programming.

Mike Hunchback

From the moment this high-school gore-hound laid eyes on the infamous Deep Red mag, it was bloodlust at first sight. I was 16, only just learning about directors like Lucio Fulci and Jim VanBebber, and still somewhat unaware of how the grisly offerings these artists slaved over fit into the cult film landscape. Deep Red's beloved founder, Chas Balun is best-loved for covering the nastiest of the nasty with cheerful joy, quick to note that even the most extreme gore effect is really a magic trick, and therefore packs a sense of wonder that we can marvel at. To say that his approach greatly influenced fandom is a crass understatement. Chas was the guy who made getting addicted to this stuff a blast. In those heady days of my youth, when everything was shiny and new, a certain film festival seemed to be coming up a lot, one that seemed like it was plugged directly into the kind of movie madness that was consuming me. Of course, I'm talking about FANTASIA: Montreal's mighty champion of indepen-

"'Well… when people ask me what I do, I tell them: I am a HORROR film journalist!'"

dent horror, Sci-Fi, exploitation, arthouse, and any other off-the-beaten-path film category you can name.

My heavenly vision of Fantasia was cemented by Alex Chisholm's remarkable fly-on-the-wall documentary In the Bel-

ly of the Beast, shot during the festival's second year in 1997, but not released until 2001. The doc gained fans as a special feature on Dark Sky's two-disc set for VanBebber's The Manson Family in 2005. In the doc, filmmakers Richard Stanley, Nacho Cerdà, Karim Hussain, and JVB waxed poetic about that year's entries, with Davis, Timpone, and Balun nearby to weigh in, as well. Filmmakers Todd Morris and Deborah Twiss debuted their kick-ass A Gun for Jennifer; without a doubt, one of the doc's highlights is Mitch Davis defending the film to a woman who seriously disapproves of the film's poster and its emblazoned, unforgettable tag-line: "Dead Men Don't Rape!"

Dreams do come true, folks. Twenty years later, thanks to the very relaunch of Deep Red you now hold in your hands, I was able to attend the fest armed with a press pass—it was an honor to say the least. The hyper-violent indie debuts that I expected were apparent—from Takashi

Deep Red staffer Mike Hunchback, lower right. Damn the Paparazzi!

Miike's elegant epic of swordplay and familial devotion Blade of the Immortal, to the stylized Game of Death, wherein insane head-explosions are met with serious laughs. Another Wolfcop provides hilarity alongside its uber-fun costuming and carnage, and Prey has veteran Dutch genreking Dick Maas showing off his skills with an onslaught of wayyy over-the-top lion attacks. Winning over audiences big-time with their bloody bad taste were Joe Lynch's Mayhem, a gore-soaked anti-corporate anthem, Trent Haaga's crazed road movie 68 Kill, and Tyler MacIntyre's brutal social satire Tragedy Girls, though no entry topped the reaction for Chris Peckover's totally twisted holiday horror flick Better Watch Out.

This year, the artier fare gave the blood and guts set a run for their money. My favorite of the fest was the supernatural (or not!?) backwoods chiller Indiana, followed by Spoor, Agnieszka Holland's humorous and moving tale of mysterious murder in the frozen rural reaches of Poland. Peter Vack's uproarious, perfectly-titled Assholes is a daringly insane, comedic slap-in-the-face, balanced by Simon Rumley's profoundly emotional Nicholas-Roeg-tribute Fashionista. And naturally, some restored masterpieces were on slate, too: Synapse's new 4K restoration of Argento's Suspiria and Arrow's immaculate treatment of Romero's The Crazies wowed audiences that had seen the films many times before, but never like this.

Amongst all this rabid film-going, I finally met Mitch Davis and crossed paths with a familiar face from NYC, Mr. Tony Timpone. Once the conversation shifted to my association with Deep Red, discussion of that lion-hearted gorehound himself, Chas Balun, was inescapable.

Mitch thought back to when he first encountered Deep Red, and the impact it had on him: "I think I was in the seventh grade or something like that. I was absolutely

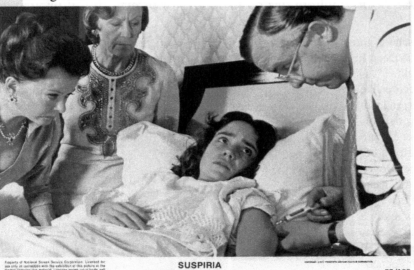

SUSPIRIA
Released by International Classics, Inc.
Prints by Deluxe®

77/133

amazed by the style, humor, and energy of Chas' writing. More than anyone else I can think of from that period, he wrote with an enthusiasm that captivated and inspired readers to jump down cinephelia rabbit holes with him, especially on the Euro-horror front. I sought out so many films and filmmakers because of his words (as well as those of the stellar stable of contributors that he put together—Steve Bissette, Graham Rae, etc.). And remember, this is pre-internet. I'd spend entire afternoons calling video stores across Montreal to ask about films, and I'd travel an hour plus, and get memberships at places just to rent a single tape from the perpetually growing Deep Red list. Of course, so many of these films either weren't available on North American home video, or were only available in recut/rescored versions that were absolute fuck-fests, so we horror kids had to write letters to all kinds of people to get the bootlegs of more complete versions. Eventually, I started buying and trading bootlegs with Chas, himself (being in French Canada, I had access to scores of Jean Rollin films that weren't yet available elsewhere on the continent, giving me primo trading ammo). I was starstruck when I got my first letter from him—he designed his own 'From the desk of Chas Balun' letterhead, from what I recall. It was like getting a letter from a rock star."

Tony recalls his first run-in with Chas: "[It was] pretty much the month I started at Fango, in July 1985. I was a fan of Chas' writing, and a copy of his The Connoisseur's Guide to the Contemporary Horror Film was sitting on my desk when I started. One of my first goals as editor was to bring Chas into the Fango bullpen, so I cold called him and asked him to write an essay on the FRIDAY THE 13th movie series. He agreed, and a great partnership was founded. I liked writers whose personality came through in their prose, and Chas truly had that.

MITCH: I finally met him in person in 1997, when he came to Fantasia. It was my inaugural year programming at the fest, and Chas was one of the first 'foreign press' that we wanted to bring in (along with Harvey Fenton, Marcele Perks, Tony Timpone, Mike Gingold, and several other writers that we admired and were excited to have here). Chas and I had several long phone chats in the months leading up to his trip, and he ended up connecting us with Jim VanBebber—he's actually the reason we ended up world-premiering the work-in-progress of The Manson Family, or Charlie's Family, as it was still titled at the time. And also Sage Stallone and Bob Murawski—they'd just struck new 35mm prints of The Beyond and Cannibal Ferox, and were in the process of launching Grindhouse Releasing. We brought them in with both prints, and the screenings were incredible. I can't believe that both Chas and Sage are gone now. It breaks my heart.

TONY: He was a larger-than-life personality. He had such a distinct voice. He had this great hippie mentality and counterculture vibe to him that was very endearing. Plus, Chas didn't have a mean bone in his body. I have very fond memories of working with him, staying at his house, partying together, and being turned on to some very cool and unusual movies by him. He is sorely missed. So many people imitate his style today that it's a real tribute to the legacy he left behind, and the influence he had.

MITCH: He was amazing. Larger-than-life, super friendly, and so much fun to discuss and debate with... his voice is terribly missed, to put it mildly.

In the name of Chas and Deep Red, I feel obligated to leave you with the one Fantasia memory that sticks out most in my mind. While we were walking to the pub after a screening, my friend Gilles Esposito, critic for the legendary French mag Mad Movies, asked me, "Why, oh why do people use the term 'genre films' so much when they simply mean horror films?" I replied thoughtfully, saying that the term "genre films" is just an expression... shorthand for what was once regulated to the B movie ghetto, from sword and sandal epics to science fiction. Gilles accepted my answer, but with intense determination replied with an answer that forever changed me: "Well... when people ask me what I do, I tell them: I am a HORROR film journalist!" After hearing it put that way, how could I ever answer differently myself?

See you at Fantasia 2018!

art by Eric Rot

KILLERFISH
FINDING SCREAMO
by: Graham Rae

A Look Back at Antonio Margheriti's Killer Fish

Graham Rae

Piranhas. Let's face it, they have a pretty bad reputation, just for being mere fish doing what comes naturally, i.e., eating meat. When you picture a piranha, you picture a nasty, nippy wee bastirt, with big fuck-off teeth, a bigger carnivorous appetite, and man-masticating malice in mind. Or, more probably, you picture a whole school of them attacking a person or animal in some inescapable frenzied underwater tornado of razor teeth and blood and screams and bubbles and slowly... dying... splashing. At least I know I do. Often. It's one of my most soothing mental images, and has helped me drift off on many a sleep-drained night.

Roll review credits. As Killer Fish starts, we are introduced to the freewheeling wheeler-dealer world of suave fucker Paul (James Franciscus, star of Argento's Cat o' Nine Tails), a gambling high roller. He had worked with animals before, in the 1976 production The Amazing Dobermans, so he is familiar working with nature's bloody snaggletooth and claw marks. Lifting a riff from the bank robbing canines from his previous production, he has set up a jewelry heist from the mining operation he used to work at, and uses gambling as an alibi.

We see the heist being performed by a small kleptomaniacal ensemble, led by Lee Majors (last seen by genre fans getting mercilessly mashed under a car's wheels in Ash vs Evil Dead), as Lasky, and Karen Black, as Kate, showcasing more of her voluptuous horror chops after appearing in the likes of Trilogy of Terror and Burnt Offerings. The several-strong group blow up a power station handily placed next to the vault they intend to rob, causing crime-covering chaos. Backed with awful back-screen projection, the explosions are cheap shite, perpetrated on a series of poor-looking (down)scale models, and it reminds you of when things went up in stuttering crackling smoke puffs in the old Thunderbirds puppet series.

No less an authority on Antonio Marghereti than Andrew Leavold, told me that the Italian director loves using models in his films and, as Andrew knows about all things diminutive in stature, what with directing the excellent midgetfest The Search For Weng Weng, I will take his word for it.

THEY SEARCH FOR TREASURE.

THEY SEARCH FOR FLESH.

KILLER FISH

The adventure that drags you in,
pulls you under and tears you apart!

SIR LEW GRADE Presents A CARLO PONTI/FILMAR DO BRASIL Production

LEE MAJORS
KAREN BLACK
MARGAUX HEMINGWAY   MARISA BERENSON in
KILLER FISH

co-starring GARY COLLINS CHARLIE GUARDINO FRANK PESCE DAN PASTORINI
and JAMES FRANCISCUS as "Paul Diller"

Music by GUIDO and MAURIZIO DE ANGELIS Screenplay by MICHAEL ROGERS
Produced by ALEX PONTI Directed by ANTHONY M. DAWSON   PG PARENTAL GUIDANCE SUGGESTED

FROM ⚡ ENTERTAINMENT   © 1979 Film Distribution   Associated Film Distribution

tain of the Cannibal God, as well as lesser worthless drivel like Death Proof. The criminals dump the emeralds in a lake and make up an arbitrary figure of 60 days to come back and pick them up, once the heat has died down, and shoot off to meet up with Paul back at the local tourist trap. There, they hang around and begin to get antsy-pantsy, and jumpy, and grumpy at the thought that somebody else could make off with the ill-gotten gains. And then, various low-rent mayhem ensues...

As you can guess, even if you've not seen it, this is one of those double-triple-quadruple-crisscross, make-you-jump films. Like Reservoir Dogs, really, but with fish, which is kind of appropriate, water-wise. It basically has some piranhas thrown in for no clear reason, except that demonizing nature for a quick exploitation buck was still acceptable in 1979, four years after Jaws first traumatized a generation of swimmers a, making everybody hate the natural world and all its manifold splendors, forever. Oh yeah, it's also a rip-off of Joe Dante's 1978 film Piranha, I forgot. Wee aquatic vicious bastirt beasties with sharp teeth were definitely in vogue 'round that time.

When I was a kid, my family spent five years in South Africa--January 1976 to December 1980. Parents would dump their preteens off at Cine Eden, the local Edenvale fleapit, on a Saturday morning, and we'd get traumatized by uncut shit like Enter the Dragon (my uncle Gary was visiting us from Scotland one time when we saw it, and was thrilled he got to see his first Bruce Lee film in a cinema), The Bees, Grizzly. and such sleaze, so it's no wonder I turned out like I did. Parents were much more liberal towards horror in the '70s, it seems, and my mother actually took myself and my brother to see this film in a cinema in Eastgate shopping centre in Johannesburg when I was 10, and my brother eight. I remember cringing at some scenes and watching through my fingers... but still watching. A beautiful memory. Try that these days and you'd get reported for child abuse. Thanks forever, maw. Seriously.

And what an exciting load of model-massacre rubbish it is! Your heart pounds and pulse races with the shit-stirring blasts of crap synth and Phantom of the Opera-like church organ at nerve-wracking, nail-chewing scenes like bolts being unscrewed from grates. Somebody should do a whole film of this stuff. They'd make a mint, and hardware stores would become the new repositories of bottomless pits of horror.

So anyway. The gang scrams to Brazil with the loot to the jaunty, screechy, gambling-themed disco hit "The Winner Takes All" (shrieked by Amii Stewart, whoever the hell she is). This huge hit, number one in South American dancefloors (sonic aphrodisiac catalyst for a thousand drunken tourista conceptions) during the late '70s, was written by Guido and Maurizio De Angelis (as was the rest of the soundtrack), music-slingers for bloodsplashers like Torso and The Moun-

Waiting back impatiently 38 years ago, the red-handed gang loll around drinking, wisecracking, and giving Lasky a chance to ponce aboot looking dapper, sweaty, and wear a sharp white hat. It's what Lee Majors (who isn't really the star in this film; it's more of an ensemble piece, where nobody truly fully has the lead spotlight) does best, so why not exploit it? An Italian-American duo of brothers in the crew, Warren (Frank Pesce—as our loyal editor John Szpunar sagely pointed out, 'Pesce' means 'fish' in Italian, so, eh…cheers, John!) and Lloyd (Charles Guardino) say they're off to Rio to chill—"When we start to boogie tonight, that plastic Jesus up on the hill is gonna hafta turn its back!" The merry boring band at the hotel is joined by a fashion shoot from New York. Margaux Hemingway (daughter of Ernest, and who also sadly ended up committing suicide) fills the stylish expensive shoes of model Gabrielle, accompanied by her rotund, bisexual photographer, Ollie (Roy Brocksmith). Ollie is actually the only character in the film who truly has character, tossing around witty waspish Wildean well-chewed bonbon mots: "Three palm trees and a lake does not Brazil make." Indeed, Ollie, indeed. The gorgeous Gabrielle clicks with the lewd Lasky. What a surprise.

But damn, who would have guessed it, those pesky brothers Warren and Lloyd decide that they're going to take a dive down to the lake and move the emeralds so that nobody can steal them. Which proves to be a rash move because, a mere third of the way through the film, we actually get to experience some piranha (in)action! Lloyd goes snorkeling… and all of a sudden, the water farts, bubbles, and turns red… he howls… and is gone. A tragic and heartbreaking scene, for anybody attending the

film and being mightily unimpressed, that is. Then, some macumba dancing crap happens on a beach for no reason. Your brain starts to head for the door. BUT WAIT! There's more! Don't leave yet! Sit back down! I promise you, it gets better! Well, sort of better… a wee bit…

Warren (Pesce), Hans (Dan Pastorini, a former pro football player, believe it or

KILLER FISH

not) another piece of shite that was part of the gang (I never mentioned him 'cus I forgot-well, who cares?), go to get the emeralds. Hans has a speargun for the "giant snake" that killed Lloyd, and goes for a rewarding swim. Predictably, he gets chomped, but manages to take his cohort with him too, by accidentally shooting him with the speargun and dragging him into the water. Lasky and Kate, out on a recon mission, manage to arrive just in time to see this crap; there is somehow not even any blood in the water this time. Fucking tragic, really, a waste of youngish treacherous human potential. Kate howls off home and Paul reveals to her that he had put piranhas in the water when he first decided to pull the job: "There must be tens of thousands by now." Just as well nobody had decided to go swimming in the lake in the interim period, eh? Suppose that would have ruined the fun. Gabrielle goes for a swim, remaining piranha-unmolested as

she is photographed. Why? Why not? Are you looking for logic here? If so…why?

Meanwhile, back at simpering kitsch central, Ollie and Gabrielle, and their small arty army, go out into the lake for a photo shoot. We just know this can't end well. Much like the film. Still, this chance of an artistic fancy feast perks our interest up a bit. Kate and Paul go to get the gems themselves (I do like that he makes the woman do the dangerous diving work—quite right!—though his ostensible excuse is that he is recovering from a heart attack), dropping some bait for the piranhas to keep them away, forgetting about the 'honor among thieves' code they have been living by until this point in the film. Kate gets freaked by a couple of cheesy gang member skeletons, but still manages to grab the gems. And finally, 53 minutes in, we see our first piranhas! And totally shitey-looking things they are too—fake as fuck, all moving in formation, clearly all tied to one wire. Worth the wait? Absolutely! It's genius! Take a look at the trailer on YouTube if you don't believe me. Who needs CGI when you have permanently-open-mouthed wastes of cardboard? Kate manages to escape with the ice anyway, though isn't best pleased when she gets out of the water, it has to be said. No sex for Paul for a while, me-thinks…whether it's good cardiac exercise or not.

The stolen gem thieves have their boat somehow trashed during a heavy rainstorm, and take refuge on the arty party's boat, fortuitously moored nearby. Handy that, eh? A cynical, laconic Lasky, invited along by Gabrielle, dubiously eyes the loot-pilfering duo, knowing what they have been up to, as he and Gabrielle play poker. Cue endless 'coded' utterances from both sides about playing games and taking advantages and such, in best Samuel Beckett fashion. Just as things are heating up between Lasky and Paul, a craply-animated hurricane hits, destroying a cheap model of a dam, which bursts. Tens of gallons of stage water spray everywhere, holing the boat on an underwater rock and running it aground near the shore.

Cue another model power station or something blowing up and getting flooded. Probably outtakes from the start that they wanted more mileage out of; who knows. Paul and Lasky have a long-overdue fight, but stop as crew members start getting chomped by piranhas in the lake. Finally, the terrible secret is out! Back on land, a kid is lightly injured by the fish in a scene boringly ripped off from Jaws. You start to keel over, weeping and drooling, but force yourself erect. You have to know how this turns out now, after sitting through 79 damned minutes of it! Death before unconsciousness, as Uncle Duke from Doonesbury put it. Though he never saw fucking Killer Fish, it has to be said. Might have changed his tune if he had. The locals dig out a single engine plane from the hurricane wreckage and take to the skies to look for survivors. Your prayers that they will crash and be eaten are, sadly, never realized.

Back on the lake, Ollie and another female member of his crew, Ann (ex-Vogue model, Marisa Berenson, probably paying for liposuction, botox injections, or something by appearing in this) decide they're going to try and make it to land , on a raft...made of wood...with holes in it. You can imagine how well that goes. His finger gets bitten and he goes overboard, and we finally get the epic, brief, semi-graphic feeding frenzy, that I recall freaking me out as a kid, that we have been waiting for, as he is torn to pieces by the merciless, ravenous, carniverous aquatic, bastirts. Red water, screaming, thrashing, piranha nibbling and gnawing a Hawaiian shirt... and a final shot of some unidentified gut matter and what looks like a cow's ribcage or something. You happy now? You finally got what you came for, 73 minutes in. Makes it feel good to be alive. Ann swims frantically to the shore, and makes it, going off to get help. The plane circles the boat and

drops a couple of rafts into the lake before crashing. Lasky swims for one and gets it, suffering only minimal bites cos he's hard as fuck. We can rebuild him! Lee Majors is invincible, everybody knows that! Not in Ash vs Evil Dead, I suppose, but, well, apart from in that... he's unstoppable!

Paul pulls a triple-quadruple-whatfuckingever cross and, waving a gun around, takes off on the raft. Lasky jumps in after him and they have a fight, with fish bait Lasky fighting from the water and Paul smashing him around with an oar. Nearly exhausted, Lasky swims back to the boat and, gushing blood, struggles and staggers

"...this is one of those double-triple-quadruple-crisscross, make-you-jump films. Like Reservoir Dogs, really, but with fish..."

aboard... clutching part of the raft he's ripped from the vessel that has allowed a wee sneaky piranha to bite a hole in it. The thieving-from-thieves thief then gets his just come-uppance, as "The Winner Takes All"—slowed down to a gentle, mournful flamenco strut—farts and warbles on the soundtrack over the frugal carnage. Franciscus, clearly not having learned his fishy lesson here, went on to star in The Last Shark in 1981, a Jaws rip-off so blatant it got successfully sued by Universal Studios for copyright infringement.

Kate appears to have gone a bit mental at the end, refusing to eat fish (oh the tedious irony) in the hospital she is in, run by, apparently, Irish nuns...in Brazil. And why not? Amazingly, a cop brings her beauty case to her, which has a false bottom, containing... guess what! Nothing. Nada. Zip. Zero. Sweet fuck all. The whole thing has been

a set-up from the start, model shoot and everything, and Ann and Lasky split the spoils of boring piranha war. Who could have seen that happening, eh? Well, nobody, cos it's utterly fucking ridiculous but, well, them's the breaks. Kate jets off into the mild blue yonder, pissed off as hell, as Gabrielle and Lasky drive off into frantic amorous oblivion, and Amii Stewart reprises inspiring waiter-on-drunken-tourist sex on the soundtrack, one final poignant time. "Lady Luck, don't let her get you down..." Would bring a tear to a glass eye.

And that, as they say, is that. Killer Fish is a strange, anomalous film, from the '70s/early '80s period when Italian exploitation filmmakers felt the need to send their finest third-rate actors and actresses into jungles to be appallingly eaten, beaten, mauled, balled, and deballed. It's anomalous in that it's not really very graphic at all, apart from the Ollie feeding scene (he would have kept those piranhas in scran for a week with that hefty, morbidly obese body!), and piranhas, whilst the stars of the advertising campaign, barely figure in it for five minutes. It's basically a slackluster heist film, with piranhas and exploding models thrown in as added spice to beef up what is a very anemic, tired, boring story.

Unless you're a piranha film completest, I wouldn't waste your time with this one; I've picked its anorexic bones apart pretty thoroughly. However, some filmmakers never learn. Japan is going to be bringing us Summer of the Piranha next year (I would guess in, eh...summer) when the worthless Piranha franchise rears its ugly, sharp-toothed wee head again. It certainly can't and won't be any better than Piranha II: Flying Killers (as it was known in the UK, which is way better than 'The Spawning'), James Cameron's finest hour (and 24 minutes). Whether or not you are masochistic or stupid enough to watch the upcoming film is entirely up to you. Me? Well, I'm staying on dry cinematic land from now on, thank you very much.

FAREWELL, BASIL GOGOS

The van Gogh of Horror

by Dennis Daniel

"Oh, no. They're dropping like flies."

That's the first thing I uttered when I received an email this morning from Deep Red Editor, John Szpunar, about the death of Basil Gogos. I'm sure it will be repeated ad infinitum by any true horror movie loving fan (especially from my generation) who grew up with Famous Monsters of Filmland magazine. It was indeed the painting of Barnabas Collins on the cover of FM #59 that first grabbed me by my pre-pubescent gonads when I was just a lad of nine, in 1969. (What issue grabbed you?)

In those bygone days, you needed a great cover to catch your eye on the magazine rack... something to pull you in. FM publisher Jim Warren knew this, and he knew he struck gold with Gogos.

When Tom Skulan asked me to edit the first edition of The Famous Monsters Chronicles back in 1990, we both knew that we'd have to track down Gogos. When we found him, he was making his living in the NYC advertising world and had not painted any monsters for many, many years. It has always been a treasured feeling in my heart that the interview in our book was the starting point for The Great Gogos to come back to the fold! Tom asked him to be a guest at FanatCon. From there, he began to show up at many horror conventions. He was in demand again to paint covers for other horror mags, and he painted some truly astonishing album covers. When I saw Rob Zombie's Hellbelly Deluxe album with the Gogos cover, I was thrilled! We got an extra 27 years of Gogos after he was rediscovered!

It's a great feeling to know that he had his renaissance! That he was able to enchant a whole new generation of fans, as well as old timers like me. He knew he was loved. He knew he was revered. What a sense of sat-

isfaction that must have given him!

And what an amazing collection of new paintings he did! Just Google his name and you'll see! He sold these prints at the conventions, and the fans gobbled them up.

Fuckin' A, Basil! Good for you!

The calling card of any true original is the one-of-a-kind nature of their work.

There is no mistaking a Gogos painting.

He told me that he would imagine that the black and white pictures that he used for reference were bathed in colored lights from all different directions. There's something very van Gogh about that style—to me anyway— hence my calling him the van Gogh of horror. This style is truly unique to Gogos. Many have imitated it since, but he was there first. And no one did it better. NO ONE.

In a Gogos painting, the monsters come alive! They literally jump into your face! They splat into your brain and burst with life!

Uncanny. Unforgettable.

I'm sure many will be singing his praises, both in print and online. Rightfully so. I can tell you that interviewing him was one of the greatest experiences I ever had. He was so kind and humble about his work. We shall not see his like again, that's for sure.

And how wonderful is it that in the new edition: Famous Monsters Chronicles II, that it was The Great Gogos himself who painted the cover! That was Tom Skulan's idea, and I can't thank him enough for securing Basil's services. It makes the book all the more precious because, as far as I know, it was the last cover he did.

One of the sad things about getting older is that more and more of the people you love and admire tend to die. I feel blessed that I met the man, and even more blessed that his work has brought me and thousands of other fans so much joy. And it will continue to do so, because his work is immortal.

I repeat...

Immortal.

PSYCHOTRONICALLY SPEAKING...

The Michael J. Weldon Interview, Part One

John Szpunar

Not long ago, I received a phone call from Deep Red staffer, Dennis Daniel. "Johnny! It's Dennis. Do you have a pencil and paper handy? I want you to call the number I'm about to give you RIGHT AWAY!" Puzzled, I picked up a pencil and acted accordingly. "Got it, Dennis. Now... what's this all about?"

Dennis paused for a minute, then said, "This, my friend, is the phone number for Michael J. Weldon. I just got off the phone

with him, and I mentioned the relaunch of Deep Red. I figured that you'd want to interview him for it—especially since you couldn't get in touch with him for Xerox Ferox. Hang up with me and call him right now. He's expecting you."

I don't know if my jaw hit the floor or not, but it's a pretty safe wager to say that it did.

The name Michael J. Weldon needs no introduction in these pages. As the original

publisher and editor of Psychotronic mag, author of The Psychotronic Encyclopedia of Film and The Psychotronic Video Guide To Film, Weldon is equal parts American original, pioneer, and legend.

One of my biggest regrets about my book, Xerox Ferox, is that I didn't have a chance to talk to Michael. The stories he could have told! I thanked Dennis for the info and dialed the number. A friendly voice answered the phone. Introductions were made, and

before long I was deep in conversation with the man. Here it is, my friends... the one that you've been waiting for! The void has finally been filled! I now present to you an in-depth interview with the one and only Michael J. Weldon!

DEEP RED: I'll start with a simple question, I guess. What kind of movies did you like as a kid?

MICHAEL J. WELDON: Well... I liked horror movies from the beginning. I was a little kid in the '50s, and before I started going to movie theaters, everything that I saw was on television. Back then, they didn't show recent movies on TV. That came later. So basically, I grew up watching movies from the '30s and the '40s. A lot of the best ones came from the Depression—features, shorts, you name it. That was the first stuff that I had access to. It was really old stuff. And horror movies appealed to me right away.

RED: Were you into comic books?

MJW: I was... for a while. I went through a typical period for kids at that time—when you're a little kid, you read Disney comics—funny animal comics. But my favorites, comic book-wise, were the DCs. Looking back on them now, the DC comics seem kind of silly. But I loved them. I was into Superman, Batman, and the Justice League. I remember Metal Men. I thought that one was really cool. [Laughs] Probably my favorites of them all were the Bizarro Superman comics.

RED: Were you exposed to the EC stuff back then, or did that come a little bit later?

MJW: No, that was before my time—they were already gone. They were banned around the time I was born. The only way

> *"I decided that I was going to do a weekly, xeroxed, hand-lettered, alternative TV Guide called Psychotronic."*

that I saw EC comics was in reprints. But I was into MAD magazine more than the comic books. I know a lot of people my age—even older—who are still heavily into comic books. I kind of outgrew them by the time I was 12 or 13. I didn't really get back into them until the undergrounds came along. But, that's another story.

RED: How about music? What really hit you back then?

MJW: Well, when I was a little kid, AM radio was all there really was. And Top 40 radio was excellent. I pretty much liked everything on the radio, and they played all types of music—you'd hear soundtrack themes, people like Frank Sinatra, Johnny Cash, Roy Orbison, and Del Shannon.

Surf music instrumentals, Motown—that kind of stuff. I just thought it was all great. Then the Beatles hit, and it got even better. I loved all of the British groups. I went through a lot of different phases—British Invasion, and then garage. The psych and the glam. It was all great.

RED: Now, you grew up in Cleveland.

MJW: That's for sure.

RED: What can you tell me about the horror hosts that were on TV in your area?

MJW: Well, the first horror host that was successful (and probably my biggest influence relating to horror movies) was Ernie Anderson.

RED: Ghoulardi.

MJW: Right. And that show started in 1963 and ended in 1966, when he moved to Hollywood. But, that show was a phenomenon in Cleveland and northeast Ohio. We watched every show that he hosted religiously. His main show was on Friday nights. He also had a movie show on Saturday afternoons. After a while, he was on every weekday showing Laurel and Hardy shorts—the early Hal Roach ones, which are great! I had already seen a lot of horror movies just kind of randomly on local TV, and then he came along. It was perfect timing, because I started reading Famous Monsters a year or two before the Ghoulardi show started. I'd read about all these movies that Forry Ackerman would go on about, and all of the sudden, Ghoulardi was showing a lot of them.

RED: Such as?

MJW: Some people look back on the history of horror hosts and just assume that they were just showing Monogram movies and the Universal classics. A lot of them did, but the Ghoulardi show was mostly showing AIP and Allied Artists movies. So, this was my first exposure to a lot of the major classic horror stars. I was just thinking about this recently. Before I saw Frankenstein or Bride of Frankenstein, I saw Frankenstein 1970. That's not a highly-regarded movie, but I thought it was great! [Laughs] I still do. I think it's a mind-blowing movie. And before I saw the Wolf Man or Mummy movies, with Lon Chaney, Jr., I saw The Indestructible Man. I could just go down the line. Before I saw the more famous Lugosi movies, I saw him in Zombies on Broadway. As a kid, it just hit the spot. I thought it was great.

RED: I'm really interested in regional horror hosts. I'm from the Metro Detroit area, and in the '70s, we had a guy called Sir Graves Ghastly. We also had The Ghoul.

MJW: OK. [Laughs] The Ghoul, of course was a spin-off of Ghoulardi. Ghoulardi had influence outside of Cleveland, which was actually amazing because he basically was a local guy. Ron Sweed used to play a gorilla on the Ghoulardi show. Some years later, when Cleveland got its first UHF channels, he basically started recreating the Ghoulardi show. He was more extreme. I mean, Ghoulardi used to blow up models. The Ghoul would blow up anything. He used some of the same music and some of the same ideas, but he added Froggy the Gremlin. Of course, I watched him, too. Meanwhile, the Ghoulardi show had been taken over by Chuck Schodowski. He was called Big Chuck. He kept the time slot going showing movies until not really that long ago. He was on for decades. It's amazing. In Chicago, they had Svengoolie. He was another knock-off of Ghoulardi. He was played by a former disc jockey named Jerry G. I used to listen to him. He was my favorite disc jockey—he was hilarious.

RED: Why do you think that the horror host thing was so popular?

MJW: Well… the horror hosts really started earlier than the ones that I saw. There was Zacherle, who I later met, and was in a TV commercial with. He started in Philly (and then New York) in the late '50s. That's when the first Shock Theater packages came out. But when Ghoulardi came along, it really was a peak period for what

you might call monster-mania. You had "The Monster Mash", which was a big hit. Famous Monsters had been around for a while, but all of the sudden, there were lots of horror magazines. You had monster albums. And, of course, around the same time, The Addams Family and The Munsters. The Hammer films had kind of brought back interest in horror characters. Monster model kits came out around the same time. Monster trading cards—there was monster EVERYTHING. I think a good illustration of how it was everywhere is the MAD magazine cover where the Frankenstein monster is making a model of Alfred E. Neuman.

RED: Oh, yeah. It's a classic.

MJW: [Laughs] Right? That was right in the center of the monster madness that was

going on. And I just loved everything about it.

RED: Yeah, you even had Beaver Cleaver wearing a monster sweatshirt.

MJW: Yes. It was such a big thing that they would even have articles about in in LIFE magazine. They'd make fun of it on sitcoms. You couldn't get enough of that stuff.

RED: That's one of the things that I've always been interested in. I've asked this question to a lot of people over the years, but I think that it's pretty important that I ask you. Why was the monster stuff so popular? Was there something in the air?

MJW: I don't have an exact answer for that, but it just fit. It came right along with the British Invasion. You had monster/horror everything and the best music ever. And

"I'd read about all these movies that Forry Ackerman would go on about, and all of the sudden, Ghoulardi was showing a lot of them."

there was more than you could take in. You couldn't buy all the good records, even if you had enough money. You couldn't see all of the movies. You couldn't watch everything that was good on TV. It was great. I loved it.

RED: What movies on the Ghoulardi show made the biggest impact on you?

MJW: Island of Lost Souls and The Hypnotic Eye!

RED: Did you ever do any writing when you were a kid?

MJW: That came a little bit later. I was briefly considered a good student, but things went downhill pretty fast. I have many theories about why that happened, but it was happening around the same time as the stuff we've been talking about. Also—you just can't leave out the fact that this was going down around the time of the Cuban Missile Crisis, and when JFK was assassinated. The Vietnam War started escalating. There was a lot of crazy stuff going on. And compared to that stuff, most of the monster stuff was nostalgic. It seemed old fashioned. And then, you also have to remember that everything was heavily censored then. In the theaters, and on TV. It's easy to have a misconception about what was available to see. That didn't loosen up

until the early '70s, maybe the late '60s. All of the sudden, they changed the ratings. It took TV a LONG time to catch up. Even after the movies started showing some blood, nudity, and some swearing... you wouldn't see that stuff on television.

RED: You mentioned Famous Monsters of Filmland. What were your thoughts on Castle of Frankenstein?

MJW: I was so into monster movies and monster movie magazines that I bought every one I could find. I bought all of the new ones that I could afford. I used to buy them at drug stores. Eventually, I discovered that there were places that sold used magazines. So, I would buy older issues of Famous Monsters that I didn't have. I bought Fantastic Monsters, Horror Monsters, Mad Monsters, and all of the other short-lived ones. But really—after a while— the best one that was commercially available was Castle of Frankenstein.

RED: What made it so special?

MJW: It was more detailed and more adult. And it was really frustrating, because it didn't come out on a regular basis at all. You just had to luck into finding it. Their publication schedule didn't make any sense at all. But as much as Famous Monsters was an influence, Castle of Frankenstein was even more of an influence, because every issue had an A-to-Z review section. They reviewed movies that you didn't have a chance in hell of seeing. Stuff that would never show up on television. A lot of European stuff. And after a while, they actually broke a few publishing taboos. All of a sudden, there was an issue of Castle of Frankenstein (this was still in the '60s) that had a feature about the new Fu Manchu movie starring Christopher Lee—he was my favorite contemporary horror star for a long time—and there were pictures of topless women in there. What's going on,

you know? [Laughs] They never would have done that in Famous Monsters! That might be part of the reason that Castle of Frankenstein ended. I don't know...

RED: Let's move along to the beginning of Psychotronic. When did you move to New York?

MJW: In the summer of '79.

RED: How and why did Psychotronic start?

MJW: Well, I can back up a little bit. My last job (after years of working horrible minimum-wage jobs, mostly in restaurants) was working at a record store. It was a lot of fun. Had more perks than benefits.

RED: This was in Cleveland?

MJW: Yes. I started working in record stores, which was a lot more fun. The last record store that I worked at in Cleveland was called The Drome. It had become, kind of by default, the place in Cleveland for punk rock. The Drome was selling Indie records, putting on shows by bands, and importing punk rock albums. When I was there, we put on shows by Devo, Pere Ubu, the Pagans, The B-52s—all that stuff. It was an exciting atmosphere. The first year I was there, the guy who owned the store— John Thompson—backed a magazine (it started out as a newspaper, really) called Cle. The editor was Jim Ellis. I did a movies-on-TV column for it. That was the first

writing that I did that anybody ever saw, outside of my notebook.

RED: How long did the mag last?

MJW: It only lasted a few issues, but that's what got me started writing the reviews that I later did a lot of. While I was still in Cleveland, I was thinking, "I want to do a magazine on my own." I did kind of a prototype—I did two of them, actually. One of them was called Pix.

RED: What was it like?

MJW: It was kind of like the prototype of

Psychotronic, but I didn't even sell it. I just made one copy for myself, just as a test. Then I did another one that was a one-shot about the films of Roger Corman. There weren't any books out yet about the films of Roger Corman. Outside of going to the library, there was no place to look up the facts. But, I got the minimal facts that I could get, and I did it.

RED: You're still in Cleveland at this point in time?

MJW: Yes. The first two times I visited New York were in '77. One of those times, I went to a—I don't know if you'd call it a film festival—but, Roger Corman was there introducing the movie I Hate your Guts.

RED: That's amazing.

MJW: [Laughs] I figure it's probably his favorite movie that he directed. I mean, most of his movies were done very quickly. And as good as a lot of them were, they were about making money. I don't think he had any hopes of making money with that one. It was more like something he needed to do. So, he was there introducing it and I met him for the first time. I gave him a copy. It was really amateurish. It looked like a kid did it. But, like I said, at the time, there were no books about Roger Corman. That came later. So, all of this was in my mind as I left Cleveland on the Fourth of July, in 1979. I loaded up everything that I wanted to take with me in a U-Haul, and just moved there by myself. I did have support when I got there, because a lot of musicians and artists moved from Cleveland to New York.

RED: Why did you move?

MJW: I loved Cleveland, but economically, it was going downhill, and the population was dwindling. It was hard to get jobs. It had just gone into default, actually. The way I look at it, I kind of went from out of the frying pan and into the fire. [Laughs] Cleveland was having a lot of problems— bad drugs were going around. Suddenly, I was in the East Village! It was more of the same. But, there was a hell of a lot more entertainment. A lot of interesting people influenced me and helped me out.

RED: What was the music scene like in New York when you got there?

MJW: Well, some people assume that it was all CBGB's, bands and punk rock. Well, that was all over with.

RED: Really?

MJW: Like... the first time I went to New

York, I went with people from that store in Cleveland, The Drome. We went to Max's Kansas City, which didn't last very long after that. We saw Pere Ubu, which I had already seen in Cleveland many times, because they were a local band. We went to CBGB's and saw Television. I loved both of those groups at the time, so that was great. When I moved to New York, I did go to CBGB's some, but most of the famous bands weren't playing there in the early '80s. Blondie and the Ramones were too big for CBGB's by that point. Other bands had broken up. So, what was going on in the music scene in New York? It was kind of fucked up, really. It was all kinds of things. Within a year or two, there was a ska revival, a rockabilly revival. And then you had the whole "No New York" thing. I knew some of the people from some of those groups. I went to high school with the drummer of Teenage Jesus and the Jerks. I'm glad that I moved to New York, and I'm glad I was there when I was, but... it was the end of a lot of things. You could still afford to live there, which you sure can't now. There was an underground music scene. There was an underground film scene going on. And there definitely was an art scene going on. So, I got to be on the fringe of all of those things. Then... it all pretty much ended, for a number of reasons. John Lennon got shot. Before you knew it, you had AIDS and crack. It was fucked up. But it was cheap! [Laughs] It was inspiring.

RED: You sort of got there near the end of the whole Times Square era, too.

MJW: I did. The theaters that I had been going to in Cleveland were closing at an alarming rate. Four theaters closed within one year. And then I go to New York. I said, "Oh my God! 42nd Street! The Deuce! This is like downtown Cleveland times ten!" And they still had cheap, affordable double and triple-bills! But within a few years, THAT had gone away. And it became what it is now.

RED: Let's get back to the birth of Psychotronic.

MJW: OK. Well, as I said, I had been toying around with doing something while I was in Cleveland, writing for Cle a little bit. I really don't know what possessed me to decide to do a weekly publication. It just seems nuts to me now. But, I decided that I was going to do a weekly, xeroxed, hand-lettered, alternative TV Guide called Psychotronic. And that's basically what it was. I subscribed to a service that would send you a printout of all the movies that were going to be on all the local New York

channels the next week. I'd go and rush, and write all of these reviews. Xerox it, staple it, collate it, and basically hand-deliver it to stores that would sell it on consignment. I mean, it was nuts. But, a lot of people seemed to enjoy it, and it got noticed. The turning point, really, was when it was written up in the Village Voice, which sadly enough just had its last print issue come out the other day.

RED: Right...

MJW: For a while, I had a girlfriend named

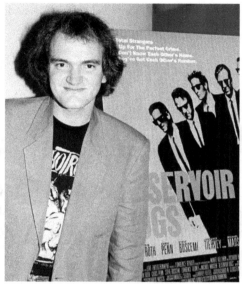

Quentin Tarantino in his trusty Psychotronic T-shirt.

"There was an underground film scene going on. And there definitely was an art scene going on. So, I got to be on the fringe of all of those things. Then... it all pretty much ended..."

Sally Eckhoff who worked at the Village Voice. She was an artist, and writer, and was very helpful. She did the typography for the Psychotronic logo. I met people at the Village Voice, including Akira Fitton, who was with Psychotronic from the beginning. He didn't work there, but I met Fred Brockman, who did all the covers for the magazine. I met Lester Bangs, who wrote a bit for Psychotronic before he died. I got to know Bob Martin, the editor (at the time)

of Fangoria. He was very helpful, and he wrote some stuff for me. The most important publicity that I got for that weekly version of Psychotronic was in the Village Voice by a writer named Howard Smith. He had directed this really cool movie called Marjoe, about Marjoe Gortner. You probably know him as an actor, right?

RED: Yeah.

MJW: He had been a childhood preacher, and it was kind of an exposé about how phony that all was. So, anyway, he wrote a whole column about my weekly xeroxed TV Guide, which somehow led to me getting a book contract.

RED: Let me backtrack a little bit. Bob Martin told me that he stayed at your apartment for a bit and that you had scrapbooks filled with clippings from monster magazines.

MJW: I did. That's kind of a story in itself. I was 10 or 11 when I really started to get heavily into the horror movie magazines. I cut them up; I made scrapbooks. I later found out that I wasn't the only person who did that. But, at one point, as I mentioned, my grades were going down and I was being told that I should go to a psychiatrist at school. My teachers told me that I was becoming a problem kid. My father, who was also a big influence on me, decided to do something about it. He did a number of things—he made me join the Boy Scouts, which I basically hated, and he made me get a job. I had to get a work permit because I was 16. He had me baptized at our church, and he threw away all of my scrapbooks. These things all backfired. Being baptized didn't change me at all. I still wanted to grow my hair long, like most guys did at that time. I started doing that, which he didn't like. I got out of the Boy Scouts as soon as possible, and I started recollecting monster movie pictures with a vengeance. I can't believe that I moved them all to New York, because there were piles and piles of them. And they were all pasted on paper from where my father worked at the Cleveland Press. They were kind of like publicity things about the circulation. I pasted stuff on the back. But, yeah. Bob stayed at my apartment, which I had for over 20 years. It was a very cheap apartment on East 9th Street. I think he stayed there when I went to Europe for the first time.

RED: Yeah, he said that you were out of town and that he really enjoyed your record collection and the scrapbooks.

MJW: He told me that he enjoyed the record collection, but I forgot that he might have looked through the scrapbooks, too.

That's great.

RED: OK. As far as the early New York zine scene goes, Bill Landis started doing Sleazoid Express around the same time that you were starting up Psychotronic. Did you know Bill at all?

MJW: I sure did. At exactly the same time, Bill Landis started Sleazoid Express, I was doing Psychotronic and Rick Sullivan [who recently passed away] was doing the Gore Gazette.

RED: Which came first?

MJW: I don't remember all of the exact dates or anything, but Bill really was the first one. And in his first issue, Rick said, "I really liked Sleazoid Express, but it's gone bad already." [Laughs] It had only been a couple issues. "I'm going to do Gore Gazette as a reaction to the stuff I didn't like in Sleazoid Express." But it was within months that all three of us started doing these fanzines.

RED: Did you get along with Bill and Rick?

MJW: I got along with both of them fine. They basically hated each other for various reasons. It amused me—I don't know how to describe it, but I was working in record stores again. Basically, doing more minimum wage work. Both of those guys were working corporate suit and tie jobs. Rick used to do all of the work for Gore Gazette at Exxon. [Laughs] He got busted for using all of their equipment. Their mailing stuff—everything. He got fired. And Bill worked at some company—I don't know what it was. But, you asked me if I knew Bill Landis. Yes, I sure did. Charlie Beesley, who was another early contributor to the first Psychotronic, had met Bill already. I think I met Bill through him. Charlie was the only person that I knew in New York that had a car.

RED: Really?

MJW: Hardly anybody had cars, unless you were rich enough to have one. It would cost you more to keep a car in a garage than to rent an apartment. He used to keep his car in the street, and the battery was always getting stolen. Charlie and I went to Bill Landis' parents' place on Staten Island and helped him move to Manhattan. That was his first apartment—he moved a bunch of times. But... he was a little bit younger than us, and he was afraid of the East Village. That's kind of understandable, if you weren't used to it. At one point, he was afraid to walk down the street. Later on, he was like a totally different person. He went through changes like I've never seen before.

RED: I can imagine. Did you know Jimmy [McDonough] at all?

MJW: I met him later on. He was buddies with Bill, and they had a falling out. I can only guess what happened. They went from working together to being rivals. I mean... Jimmy McDonough's done some major stuff. He did the Shakey book on Neil Young. He's got a new book out about Al Green.

RED: He wrote the best biography that I've ever read—The Ghastly One—about Andy Milligan.

MJW: [Bill and Jimmy] became rivals, and they both wanted to do books on Kenneth

TWO ZANIES ON A ZOMBIE HUNT!
WALLY BROWN ALAN CARNEY BELA LUGOSI in ZOMBIES ON BROADWAY
with ANNE JEFFREYS • SHELDON LEONARD • FRANK JENKS
Produced by BEN STOLOFF • Directed by GORDON DOUGLAS • Screen Play by LAWRENCE KIMBLE

Anger. They both wanted to do books on Andy Milligan. I don't know what went down between them, but I think the fact that Bill basically became a junkie who was acting in porno movies must have had something to do with it.

RED: It probably did.

MJW: But Bill... I just want to say one more thing. He introduced me to a lot of people, and he did nice things. He leant me pictures for my first book. And also, Bill, Rick Sullivan, and myself did film shows in New York.

RED: You know... not to veer back, but Bob Martin was telling me about a woman who had some kind of monster society in New York. Do you remember anything about that?

MJW: Well, sure! Besides 42nd Street and Times Square (which were amazing), there were a number of still-operating theaters in the East Village. Double-bill midnight movies and stuff. Along with them was a club in the basement of a church called Club 57.

RED: OK...

MJW: They had a weekly thing called the Monster Movie Club. It was only a block away from where I lived. This place is known to some for the artists that hung out there, but I usually went there for the movies. Charlie Beesley showed some movies there, Bill Landis showed some movies there, and Rick Sullivan, too. They showed a lot of films that I'd already seen, but that was the first place that I saw Two Thousand Maniacs.

RED: What was the place like?

MJW: It was a cool semi-private basement club. The lady who was most in charge of showing the movies was named Susan Hannaford. I've been in touch with her recently on Facebook. I don't know, but I think she might be working on a book about the place.

RED: Hopefully so.

MJW: There's a lot of interest about that time period in New York City. There will probably be a book about that place, eventually. In fact, A Club 57 exhibit is currently on display at The Museum of Modern Art (MOMA)—including copies of zines from Landis, Sullivan, and me.

RED: As far as your first book goes, how did that come about?

MJW: Well, it had a lot to do with me doing that original Psychotronic weekly thing and getting written up in the Voice. One person who saw the Voice article was Christopher Cerf. He had been heavily involved in National Lampoon at one time. Even now, he's known for the many books that he's written and for working on Sesame Street.

RED: [Laughs]

MJW: It's kind of a funny thing, but it's what it is. He and a Texas oil billionaire friend of his came to my tiny little apartment to meet me. I got to hang around with them for a while. If you didn't know, his father owned or started Random House/Ballantine books. [Laughs] His father used to be a regular on the What's My Line? show. I used to watch his dad a lot as a kid. So, that's really how I got the first book contract. It was through him. I quickly realized that I couldn't concentrate on doing an actual book and doing a weekly publication at the same time. So, I regretfully stopped the publication and started doing a lot of research...

TAPE CUTS

Part two of this exclusive interview will continue in the next issue of Deep Red!

AN END TO HORROR: CAUTIONARY TALES

Fond Memories of Chas & Less Fond Experiences with Others
Stephen R. Bissette

Part the First—In Which I Sing the Praises of a Late and Lamented and Sorely-Missed Friend and Fellow Traveler, He Who First Opened the Door to My Scribed Accounts, Interviews, Screeds, Rants, and Reviews; And a Brief But Loving Farewell to Said Late and Lamented Friend and Mentor, And How He Established the Firm and Sound Foundations Upon Which the Publication You Hold Now Were Constructed, and Its Editor and Publisher and Contributors Now Labour to Honor and Adhere To, Even to Expand Upon, for the New Century We Are All Amid, Whatever Our Individual States of Affairs or Situations.

If you wonder why I still work with fanzines (at present, zines like **Monster!**, **Weng's Chop**, and this revival of **Deep Red** you're reading), trustworthy publishers like Black Coat Press and Crossroad Press, and have returned to self-publishing with a vengeance as of this year,[1] rather than free-

1 The new SpiderBaby Grafix & Publications

lance for the mainstream magazine market or work more diligently to prime pumps in the mainstream book market—read on, and wonder no more.

> *"Fuuuuuck, Bissette, I do all my books the old-fashioned way, paste-ups and mechanicals with stats, glue-gun, waxer, and boards; so much for these fucking computers! This book's a fucking mess!"*

self-publishing effort was launched on November 3, 2017 with the publication of my new book *S.R. Bissette's Cryptid Cinema™ : Meditations on Bigfoot, Bayou Beasts & Backwoods Bogeymen of the Movies*, available at https://www.amazon.com/dp/1975938135/ref=nav_timeline_asin?_encoding=UTF8&psc=1

As ever, zine work is a labor of love. We do it for no money—though there are exceptions to that—usually for barter (comp copies of issues we're in), at best. But we retain ownership of our work, leaving us free to compile our work into books that we also own. It's a form of creative economy and cottage-industry publishing. When we work for mainstream magazine and/or book publishers, though, we are paid (magazines usually pay flat 'per article' rates, book publishers usually pay what we laughingly call "advances").

As a freelancer with four full decades under my belt, I've many a tale to tell, and I thought I'd share with you some of the conversations I had with the late great Chas Balun in what turned out to be the last few of years of Chas' time with us on this Earthly plane of existence.

Chas, aka: Charlie, had been fighting cancer as long as I knew him (we first met in the late 1980s), and his 2009 skirmish in the ongoing war took him. Even given his sturdy frame, radiation treatments and chemo took a toll every battle Charlie had with the disease (radiation and chemo was, in Charlie's words, "like deer-hunting with napalm, dude: you torch the entire fucking mountain trying to take out one little buck").

Charlie was, literally, a Viking of a man: huge, hearty, often hilarious, always deadly honest and absolutely full of life. He changed my life for the better from the moment we first communicated—Charlie was the first editor (with *Deep Red*) to open the door to my writing career—and though we rarely got to get together in the flesh (Vermont was a little too "hill people" life for Charlie and Pat, and his and Pat's Los Angeles area base sure is a looooooooong ways away, though I did get to visit them a couple of times over the years), Charlie was both a beacon and an anchor in good and tough times for me, personally and creatively. I love the man still, and I miss him terribly; life is leaner without Charlie.

Even at the worst of times, Charlie kept his spirit and his wicked sense of humor. Among our last email exchanges is this characteristically candid reply:

"–Sorry it's been sooooooooo long, my friend. Going thru yet another bout w/ cancer (which has returned with a metastasizing fury and spread) and trying hard to keep my wits about me. Finished w/ radiation and nearly done w/current chemo. Have a CT scan this week to check on things. It has not been pretty. Had surgery a few months ago but they decided to pursue other approaches in the future because of the spread and location of the bad mojo. It SUCKS, really does. Taking it one day at a time and still hoping for blue skies. Hope all is well with you & yours, ol' buddy.

Peace,

The Chazmanian Devil"

Now, a lot of folks cried when the news of Charlie's passing circulated. A lot of crocodile tears spilled, too, from folks who maybe should have done right by Charlie when they were in a position to do so. A sobering note was ignored amid all the eulogies that followed Charlie's passing. As I wrote the day I'd been told of his death,

"I have to note that during the last decade or so whenever Charlie and I got to talking about getting work into print he didn't have too many kind words for the state of either fan or pro publishing. His last couple of book projects ended badly; one remains unpublished, though the finished book (Charlie always turned in complete camera-ready boards) has malingered for well over a decade."[2]

For what it's worth, Charlie's final book, **Beyond Horror Holocaust: A Deeper Shade of Red** (Fantasma Books, 2003),

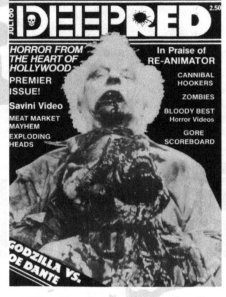

"Sadly, many who built careers of their own on copping Charlie's attitude (but never his candor or wit) never gave Charlie his due…"

was published the very year the events I'm about to relate to you (in Parts the Second and Third) went down. If nothing else, both experiences gave us a lot to talk about.

From his first self-published chapbook **The Connoisseur's Guide to the Contemporary Horror Film** (1983), Chas forever changed how folks wrote about the genre. Sadly, the very successors who 'adopted' the tenor and tone that was originally Charlie's alone and built careers of their

own on copping Charlie's attitude (but never his candor or wit) never gave Charlie his due, or made it possible for him to get his final dream projects into print, either. Fuck 'em; they'll never hold a candle to the man, and they've missed any chance they ever had to repay their debt to him.

Much as Charlie loved horror movies, his sentimental streak was shamelessly miles long; he was a sweet bear of a fellow, really. Among his favorites films was the movie **Ring of Bright Water** (1969, from the 1960 non-fiction novel by Grant Maxwell), and he called me in 2008 when I sent him a package of memorabilia from that classic animal-lovers gem, and his and Pat's home was adorned with more than one of Charlie's expansive paintings of otters and the animals he loved—hanging right next to amazing horror movie props from his pals at KNB.

Charlie deeply loved his wife Pat, their pets, his music, his guitar, his art, his home, his weed, his life. He didn't care much for the bullshit of doing business in this sorry world, but he made his way as a freelancer.

Now, few comics historians note the fact that Chas was among the real 1980s pioneers of the minicomics form.[3] Almost nobody talks about Charlie's comix work—his collaborative minicomic ventures with his pal George DiCaprio (father

2 This quote, and portions of this Part the First, were originally published on my blog *Myrant*, "Sad News Ends 2009: To My Friend Chas Balun…", December 31st, 2009, archived online at http://srbissette.com/sad-news-ends-2009-to-my-friend-Chas-balun/ , and "The Forgotten Chas Balun Comix: Minicomics from the Lord of Gore Score," January 26, 2010, archived online at http://srbissette.com/Chas-balun-comix/

3 The best of all published minicomics histories to date is Bruce Chrislip's *The Minicomics Revolution, 1969–1989* (self-published, July 2015). George DiCaprio is mentioned once, on only one page (pg. 346), Chas and Chas' minicomics aren't mentioned at all.

of famed actor Leonardo). Charlie told me George (who Chas caricatured as "Jorge") made part of his living as a distributor of comix and such to head shops and bookstores, which led to their collaborating on these minicomix and the like. Charlie gifted me with a few copies over the years, and I treasure 'em. He never ceased in expressing his amazement at the amount of comics and comix work I'd done over the years—and he couldn't stomach anyone dissing me for being 'slow' at it.

One of my fondest memories of Chas is the spectacle of him not-too-gently tearing into a mouthy comic fan at a convention we were both at; "You have no fucking idea how much work this man has done! Have you ever in your fucking life drawn just one page of comics, dude? You should be kissing Bissette's fucking feet!" Chas being Chas, he didn't mince words—but he wasn't a bully about it, either, and the kid came back to buy one of everything we had at the table later, and ended up having a nice chat with both of us. That was Chas for you.

Charlie thought anyone who did comix for anything but the love of it had no idea what they were in store for—and he was right. "Fuck, Bissette, you're fucking crazy! Comix are just too hard, way too much work!" he'd laugh, and he knew the ropes personally from his own minicomics creations. Between Tom Skulan and me, we managed to coax a cover and a story or two out of Chas for *Gore Shriek*, but Chas only did so out of love for the medium. After each comix gig, he'd swear, "Fuck that! Back to illustrations and T-shirt art for me! Just one drawing and it's done, man, and it pays waaaaay better!" Ain't it the truth.

Now, about Charlie's minicomics: *Spaz* #2 (I never saw #1) is the earliest of Chas' comix in my collection (all personalized to me), dating from 1977. This places Chas (and uncredited publishing partner George) in the Clay Geerdes generation of underground minicomics cartoonists, the generation vet undergrounder Larry Todd (*Dr. Atomic*) once declared the true successors to the original underground comix movement of the 1960s and early '70s. Chas called his comix operation 'Duck Studios' and kept at it into at least 1980, a couple of years before his undying love for horror movies steered him toward self-publishing the chapbooks and collaboratively

publishing the first issue of *Deep Red* as a pretty slick zine. *Mighty Spazzy* was published in 1979, and here's the full cover spread—front cover on the right, back cover (*Pachuco Romance*) on the left. *A Day in the Life of Mr. Hostile* followed in 1980.

I remember Chas showing me at least a couple others during one of my two visits to his and Pat's home, but I don't recall what those comix were titled; I was pretty overwhelmed with the sheer diversity of Chas' incredible skills as an artist, from his minicomix to his oversized painted canvases (primarily animal portraits, but there were also some pop-art-like works for clients and commissions that were mighty

"Fuck, Bissette, you're fucking crazy! Comix are just too hard, way too much work!"

gorgeous, too!).

Charlie never suffered fools for long, and always called a spade a spade, regardless of how the chips might fall. There's so many stories—yes, it's true that Charlie was ratted out to the FBI in a chain of events that began with idiot Charlie Sheen calling the authorities when he was grossed out screen-

ing a video boot of Hideshi Hino's notorious Japanese *Guinea Pig* faux-'snuff' film *Za ginipiggu 2: Chiniku no hana/ Flower of Flesh and Blood* (1985); being an old hippie, Chas was outraged (and it was Chris Gore, *Film Threat* founder and cine 'bad boy', who narced!), and according to Chas one of the first things he said to the agents at his door was, "Did any one of you watch the end of the fucking video?" Jesus H. Christ, the 'Making of' short was right there, showing how the special effects illusions were fabricated. D'oh!

In the final year of Chas' life, the "mainstream" mainstay of genre journalism, *Fangoria*, was busily stiffing its freelancers with relative impunity. We'd not only seen it coming, we'd already been through it. Sometime after the demise of *Fangoria*'s short-lived companion magazine *GoreZone* (launched 1988, running 27 issues; there was another even shorter-lived companion, *Toxic Horror*, running only five issues), freelancers for both magazines received letters on the publisher's stationary saying, in so many words, that whatever prior agreements we'd had with the publisher, *Fangoria* was now instituting a "retroactive work-for-hire" agreement with all freelancers, turning over all ownership to the publisher. A one-page contract was attached, with no offer of additional payment for this "retroactive" appropriation of copyright. Now, a few things you need to know: (1) *Fangoria* paid freelancers upon publication, not acceptance, of work, so sometimes you waited months, as long as a year, for payment; (2) $200 was the most I ever knew *Fangoria* to pay for anything; (3) under the terms of United States Copyright laws, circa the 1990s, "retroactive work-for-hire" wasn't legal or even possible—"work-for-hire" (meaning, the employer/publisher is legally the author of the work, and owns copyright) only fit very specific venues of publication, and had to be asserted and contracted at the time of assignment.[4] In the case of my "With My Eyes Peeled" column in *GoreZone* (where Chas' "Piece O'Mind" column also appeared) and my meager contributions to *Fangoria*, I had in fact specifically negotiated with editor, Tony Timpone, as a

4 Hell, don't take my word for it: see "Work Made For Hire Agreement Cannot Be Retroactive," http://www.mosessinger.com/articles/work-made-hire-agreement-cannot-be-retroactive

condition of working with the magazines, my retaining my copyright on my work—it was right there, in print, on the first page of every "With My Eyes Peeled" column entries. When a Brazilian fan mailed me a copy of the Brazilian edition of *GoreZone* with my column in Spanish, my copyright in place, sans negotiation or payment to me, I had words with Tony. For that, and other reasons I won't go into here, we agreed to terminate my employ with *GoreZone*. Soon afterwards, the "retroactive work-for-hire" letter arrived, which I refused to sign (as did a number of my friends who also freelanced for *Fango* and *GoreZone*). Bad blood was the result, sadly, between the publisher and those of us who said 'no.'

After that damned "retroactive work-for-hire" letter, Chas and I had moved on, but we kept tabs as best we could on what was going down in the field. As far as much of the horror fan field and cottage industries went, Chas felt spent and ill-used at times, and expressed his despair during our rambling phone conversations. He was profoundly displeased with the botched misprinting of his book *Gore Score 2001: The Splatter Years* (Obsidian Books, November 2000), a casualty of early-in-the-digital-production-era small-press publishing; the book was riddled with errors, with pages out of order, mismatching captions and photos throughout, and rendering much of the book almost unreadable. Unable to afford a corrected replacement print run, the young publisher tried to make good—I facilitated a final delivery of boxes of the print run to Chas, picking them up in my car, in Syracuse, NY and shipping them to Chas myself—but it really bummed Chas out. Chas printed up an "errata" insert sheet and we'd already done a signature plate featuring one of my zombie drawings, with both of us signing 'em all in blood-red ink, but the bloom was off that sorry little rose. "Fuuuuuck, Bissette, I do all my books the old-fashioned way, paste-ups and mechanicals with stats, glue-gun, waxer, and boards; so much for these fucking computers! This book's a fucking mess!"

Nevertheless, Charlie was the loyalist of amigos. He maintained his loyalties with those he trusted and those who proved trustworthy, working with Shawn Lewis's Rotten Cotton operation to the end. It still made Charlie happy to see his friends in the industry make the occasional breakthrough; Dave Parker was one of Chas' filmmaker friends, and Chas was a booster. I got to meet him during one of my visits to California to see Chas and Pat, and Chas was always glad to share good news about how Dave was making his way as best he could, for instance: "You two should get along," Chas smiled before taking me to the little gathering I'd met Dave at, "you're both hill-people!" (Sure enough, Dave heralded from Richmond, VT, about 15 miles from where I'd grown up). Charlie also wasn't shy about expressing his sorrow, sometimes despair, and occasional disgust for those former friends who hit hard

THE GORE SCORE

Ultraviolent Horror in the 80's

by Chas. Balun

❖❖❖ REVISED & UPDATED ❖❖❖

"I've had it with even trying to cover these bullshit movies, or try to say something new when all anyone cares about are these bullshit remakes."

times, those who hit the bottle too hard, or those who betrayed Charlie's trust (primarily those who let success of any kind go to their heads "and act like a fucking asshole to the little people who got 'em where they are, or think they are"). I can hear Chas' voice now: "Fuuuuuuck, Bissette, who needs that?"

"Nothing even makes me think about going back to it, Bissette," Chas said one evening. "I'm much happier just painting my paintings, doing my little T-shirts for Shawn, now and again. I've had it with even trying to cover these bullshit movies, or try to say something new when all anyone cares about are these bullshit remakes, then not get paid for my troubles. Who needs it? Fuuuuuccck. You know what I'm talking about, Bissette, after all we've been through. You've been in deeper trenches then I have; we've been there and back. Shit, man! Life is just too fucking short."

Life is too fucking short, indeed.

I thought of Chas saying that time and time again in the years after his passing.

Then again, Chas and I had no illusions going into our working relations with newsstand magazines like *Fangoria* and *GoreZone*. We'd each had our respective experiences with how these businesses worked, and few things surprised us.

The same isn't true for others; there's still a generation that grew up reading *Fangoria* and still foster grand illusions about how "cool" it might be to write for such a legendary venue.

Josh Hadley is among the most recent procession of *Fangoria* magazine freelancers. "*Fangoria* was a magazine I grew up with and was more or less my bible," Josh explained to me. "To think that years later I would get to write for them and to see my words (and my name) in the pages of a magazine I held so dear was amazing." The reality, though, was something altogether different:

"Sadly, by the time I got involved, *Fangoria* was not the magazine I had once revered. Now it was full of shady tactics, vapid people, and worst of all, an owner that would make every corporate sleaze juice themselves…. How I got to write for them is such an odd story. I had been reading *Fangoria* since the early 1980s and had many years' worth of subscriptions along with simply buying the issues off the newsstand. I kind of gave up around the early 2000s when I felt the magazine had hit its lowest point—that *Twilight* cover. It was not *Fangoria* any longer.

I ran across a random issue in a used

store a few years later and found the magazine had really rebounded. Seems there had been an editorial change and Chris Alexander (formally of **Rue Morgue**) was really making the magazine something once more. Then Alexander had something of a controversy hit him. Seems he reviewed his own film using a pseudonym[5] in a magazine he edited without telling the readership. I took issue with that. After the [Lianne] Spiderbaby [MacDougall] plagiarism scandal[6] I went after **Fangoria** and Alexander hard on my radio program, and in a column I used to write for a website which I am no longer part of. Alexander messaged me and we got to talking, and even though I was not comfortable with what he had done, he asked me if I wanted to pitch something. I hit him with a few ideas and one really stuck: a look at the movies that you can only get on VHS tape; those movies that, for one reason or another, are in a legal purgatory keeping them off DVD. This was a 2-page one-off article. It seems it went over quite well with the readership and I was asked if I wanted to turn it into a regular column. So, I began writing that column every issue along with some special assignments for the magazine (looking at the Kevin Smith produced **Vulgar** film or reviewing books that pertained to VHS culture). I got the job by insulting and attacking the editor-in-chief of the magazine. Not a style I recommend but it somehow worked. I should [have] had my radar up at that time but I was too blind to see it."[7]

Keeping one's blinders in place is a freelancing survival skill that can backfire. Veteran **Fangoria** freelancer Phil Nutman and I were friends to the end of Phil's life, and to the end we stayed in touch via the phone and (only at times) via "Assbook" (Phil's contemptuous moniker for Facebook so-

cial media, which he loathed). Phil was finally successfully co-scripting and producing movies—proudest of all of his Jack Ketchum (nom de plume of mutual friend Dallas Mayr, who also was pals with Chas) adaptations, particularly **The Girl Next Door** (2007), and of his last effort, a short film adaptation of Elizabeth Massie's terrifying short story **Abed** (2012)—but Phil was still dependent on the occasionally freelance gig, including work for **Fangoria**. This proved to be a constant frustration once it came time to be paid. Phil loved **Fango** and (like Chas) had only kind words for **Fangoria** editor, Tony Timpone, as did most in the field, but Phil often voiced his

"I still work with fanzines (at present, zines like Monster!, Weng's Chop, and this revival of Deep Red you're reading), trustworthy publishers like Black Coat Press and Crossroad Press..."

complete ire and despair with **Fangoria**'s late—or complete lack of—payment for work he'd taken on, which Tony would make good on when the publisher didn't, which drove Phil nuts.[8]

Phil was hardly alone. Mike Watt said of Chas Balun, "Chas was one of the first pros who reached out to me during my nascent years as a horror critic. Encouraging, funny, surprising. Our friendship was cut too short, too quickly. I miss him." [9] Like Phil Nutman and Josh Hadley, Mike was one of the many freelancers who struggled to maintain sane relations and work with **Fangoria**, despite shoddy treatment. When assigned by still-editor Tony Timpone to cover the filming of **Sorority Row** (the nominal remake of the 1983 **The House on Sorority Row**), Mike "almost didn't accept the assignment":

"It's 2009 and **Fangoria** still owed me money for the set-visit I did the previous year, for **My Bloody Valentine 3-D**. **Valentine** had been... not quite a nightmare, but an unpleasant experience.... We were in a dank mine, none of the stars were on call that day, something that annoyed my editor, Tony Timpone. Worst of all, for me at least, was that I had to 'share' my visit time with a self-described 'trust fund asshole' who worked as an online blogger for some now-defunct horror site. He also admitted to everyone who was in earshot, that his only reason for being there [on the set of **My Bloody Valentine 3-D**] was to ask out [the film's co-star] Jaime King. He knew he didn't have a shot, said he, but he'd be damned if he didn't try. The rest of the time he spent trying to impress [director Patrick] Lussier on his horror knowledge. He never asked a question, just interrupted the answers.

That **Fango** was delinquent was no fault of Tony's. Rest assured, I was in good company of the unpaid. I managed to get a personal guarantee of payment from Tony, though at a much lower rate, which suggested to me this marker was coming out of his own pocket and that alone was enough to get me to capitulate…"[10]

But I'm getting ahead of the chronology

5 .Alexander's *nom de plume* was "Ben Cortman." The controversy was over Alexander/"Cortman" writing about (and "interviewing" Alexander) Chris Alexander's own movie, *Blood for Irina* (2012), in *Fangoria* #319 (January 2013).
6 See Alex Ballingall, "Quentin Tarantino's Toronto girlfriend accused of plagiarism: Lianne 'Spiderbaby' MacDougall, a U of T graduate, apologizes on Twitter and says she's stepping away from horror movie journalism," thestar.com, July 15, 2013, archived online at https://www.thestar.com/entertainment/movies/2013/07/15/quentin_tarantinos_toronto_girlfriend_accused_of_plagiarism.html ; also see Richard Horgan, "After Plagiarism Victory Over Lianne Spiderbaby, This Writer Isn't Celebrating," *AdWeek*, July 15, 2013, archived online at http://www.adweek.com/digital/maryann-johanson-flick-filosofer-plagiarism-lianne-spiderbaby/
7 Josh Hadley, November 5th, 2017 email to the author; quoted with permission.

8 Alas, Phil tragically perished too soon—age 50 years, a victim of alcoholism—on October 7, 2013.

We'd last spoken in August of that year. Tony Timpone's heartbreaking *Fangoria* obit is still archived online at http://www.fangoria.com/new/remembering-philip-nutman-1963-2013/ ; as Tony writes, "He never missed a deadline, always filed the "big pieces" that stood out as issue anchors…He sent in at least 120 feature articles over three decades, right up to *The Walking Dead*…"
9 Mike Watt, Facebook comment to my own page, November 5, 2017; quoted with permission.
10 Mike Watt, "Padding Pages Department: A Forced Death March of Memory Down SORORITY ROW," *Exploitation Nation #2* (2017, Happy Cloud Media, LLC), pp. 13–14; quoted with permission.

here, aren't I?

Chas succumbed to cancer just before Christmas of 2009; December 18th, 2009, to be precise.

In our phone conversations, Chas was philosophical about his health situation to the end. If there was anything he expressed bitterness about to me, time and time again, it was the treatment meted out as a matter of course to freelancers—freelancers like Mike Watt. Freelancers like Phil Nutman. Freelancers like ourselves.

"Shit, Bissette, you'd think our having so many years under our belts would mean something," Chas said at one point. "All I'm tasting is shit in my mouth!"

Then, that laugh of Chas', punctuating the only sane response possible.

Sometimes, all you can do is laugh.

***

Part the Second—Being At This Juncture Less of an Eulogy to a Beloved Friend and Mentor, But Rather a Chronology of Some Length, Concerning That Which My Friend and Mentor and I Commiserated About Nearly to the End of His Days, As Well as Chronicling as Evidence of Our Discourse That Which Did Not "Work Out," to the Loss of Only the Author, Punctuated with Some Fits of Humour and Passages of Slight Sorrow, and Ending Without Resolution, Save for Dissolution and Some Sorrows.

As all good gorehounds know, Charlie Balun aka Chas Balun changed everything about how horror movies were weighed, valued, and written about with two self-published chapbooks in 1983 and '84. *The Connoisseur's Guide to the Contemporary Horror Film* was published first, in 1983; *The Gore Score* was self-published by Chas the following year. The first was dedicated to his beloved wife Pat. These were slim, modest, tidy chapbooks—32 pages + covers, selling for just $3.95. But it's *The Gore Score* that really rang bells for horror fans and gorehounds, enjoying subsequent printings and editions after FantaCo Enterprises proprietor and publisher, Tom Skulan, bought up the entirety of Chas' remaining print run to sell via FantaCo's mail-order division and arranged for a FantaCo expanded and re-

vised edition to be published. *The Gore Score* changed everything.

That's the first thing you've got to understand completely before I share the following…

About 13 years ago (2004), my misadventure with one of the few slick horror mags then remaining on the newsstand only demonstrated anew to Chas and me that (1) having "credentials" adds up to squat, save for flattery, and (2) even the best intentions and most diplomatic of exchanges may indeed add up to squat. Neither of which is the 'moral' of the story, because as far as I can ascertain, the only moral is the usual: the gigs go to the bullpen writers and/or friends of the editor, however professional,

"*Having edited and published as well as freelanced over my years in the biz, I've been on all sides of the process.*"

flexible, outgoing, forthcoming, and accommodating one tries to be.

'Cold call' submissions used to be a rather clumsy exercise, involving either literal 'cold calls' via telephone accompanied, preceded, or followed by a 'cold' (unsolicited) submission via snail-mail. Email and the internet has made this a far less clumsy

process, in that one can submit introductory letter and submission all at once in a close enough proximity to real time that both author and editor can see through the transaction quickly and with greater efficiency than before. This avoids wasting time for either party, and if the end result is rejection, it's over quickly for all concerned. This is a good thing in all ways, as nothing is worse (for either party) than the mounting of false expectations—but I'm getting a bit ahead of myself here.

Having edited and published, as well as, freelanced over my years in the biz, I've been on all sides of the process. As an editor, this occasionally yields some delightful material amid the 'slushpile'—the industry term for the heaps of unsolicited material that inevitably arrives and accumulates, however diligently one attends to the daily mail. 'Slushpile' also succinctly describes the nature of much unsolicited material that arrives, so I knew from experience (again, on both sides) that my best 'cold call' effort should always include a coherent, comprehensive introductory letter. Having a few credits to my name, it can't and usually doesn't hurt.

That said, it's extremely rare that I 'cold call' any longer. Thankfully, work offers arrive often enough to carry me over most months, even with me saying 'no' to almost 100% of the comics-related inquiries. The rare exception comes, usually, when I find myself quite enjoying a given publication with some regularity, and thinking (in my weak moments), "Hey, maybe it would be fun and/or profitable to write something for these folks, see if they'd have me aboard."

Which leads me to this narrative, which I will relay to you as a chronology of exchanges, just as it happened. Sometimes, one begins something thinking "maybe we can do business together," only to arrive at "let me see how long this takes to play out."

In the spirit of protecting the guilty, however innocent, I'll not indulge names—only dates—unless it's to do with my efforts from my end of the exchange. I'll also keep my quoting emails from the magazine editor to a minimum, just including enough to cover the chronology of events.

It began with a phone call, which seemed to have been received warmly.

Having thus broken the ice, the phone conversation was followed immediately by an email, and an attached, complete 'cold' submission:

From: Marge & Steve Bissette [mailto:msbissette@yahoo.com]

Sent: October 21, 2003 4:35 PM

To: -----

Subject: Steve Bissette following up phone call w/review for GHOSTS

Dear ------,

Hope this finds you both well. Steve Bissette here, the fellow who drew Alan Moore's *Swamp Thing,* co-created and co-published *Taboo,* and did everything on *Tyrant™* and *SpiderBaby Comix* while writing for *Deep Red, Video Watchdog, Ecco, Fangoria, GoreZone* and many other zines. Forgive the blunt American aggression, but I'm eager to contribute to your fine zine.

As a longtime reader of --------, I'm being a bit bold here and contacting you both out-of-the-blue with a review submission. I recently had the opportunity to see Stefan Avalos' *The Ghosts of Edendale*, and am hoping to find a suitable home for my review.

I'm attaching it as a text document and cut-and-pasting it into this letter, below. I'm no shill for the filmmakers, but I do love the film. I have taken the precaution of ensuring they could provide photos and such if you accept this submission: contact _____ at _____ or at: [email contact]

If you don't pick this up, no sweat. Just let me know what you're take is; I'm offering it to -------- first, and hope to keep my foot in the door for more writing, if you're open to such a thing.

My contact info:

[contact info followed]

Thanks!

All the best, always,

Steve B

Here's the complete original review I sent along, with no idea of the magazine's parameters (word count, etc.)—just placing something complete into their hands, as strong a first volley as an author can give.

It was a sample, an offering, a submission, if you will:

THE GHOSTS OF EDENDALE (2003)

The California Gold Rush never ended. Evocative yarns of dead 'old Los Angeles' spreading its clammy presence into 'new Los Angeles' are as old as the Hollywood hills, spawning non-supernatural noirs (*Chinatown*), geriatric gothics (*Sunset Boulevard*, *Whatever Happened to Baby Jane?*, etc.), bewitching nightmares (the *Thriller* episode "A Wig for Miss DeVore," *Mulholland Drive*), and at least one bonafide literary classic, Nathaniel West's "The Day of the Locust." There's ghosts and 'bad fuggums' (to quote Captain Beefheart) in

"Even the best intentions and most diplomatic of exchanges may indeed add up to squat."

them thar hills, and they're forever hungry to reclaim lost glories, withered beauty, and squandered youth. 'They' feed on irrational dreams of untapped riches, elevating celebrity, and virtual immortality that draws generation after generation to Tinseltown likes incendiary moths to the flame. And like moths, the intimate apocalypses that most often result provide the brief, fleeting spectacle of lives, loves, and dreams gone up in spirals of smoke.

Building on the accomplishments of his

debut feature *The Money Game* (aka *The Game*, 1994) and his collaborative work with Lance Weiler on the pioneer digital feature *The Last Broadcast* (1998), writer-director-editor Stefan Avalos crafts his own spin on this archetype with the eerie, unsettling *The Ghosts of Edendale*. Basing his latest feature on uncanny personal experience—*Ghosts* is set in Avalos' adopted L.A. neighborhood, filmed in his own home—and working hand-in-hand with producer Marianne Connor (*Impressions of Jordan*, *Time 'til Light*) and a most capable cast and production team, Avalos once again embraces digital technology to mount an chilling gem which taps an almost-palpable, suffocating sense of dread.

We first meet Kevin (Stephen Wastell, of *The Money Game* and *The Miner's Massacre*) and Rachel (Paula Ficara) as they move into their 'dream house' in old Hollywood's historic Edendale, the bedrock of the movie capital's silent-era beginnings. Their plan is to tap the promised wellsprings, writing and selling screenplays to carve out a new life for themselves, far from a fleetingly-sketched troubled past in the East. Kevin cottons immediately to the place, intrigued by its history and happy to find all their neighbors (including Keith Fulton and Louis Pepe, the masterminds behind the documentaries *The Hamster Factor and Other Tales of Twelve Monkeys* and *Lost in La Mancha* share his interests in working on and in the movies. Rachel, however, is almost immediately confronted with a 'second sight' of Edendale's underbelly, and it is her swelling fear which shapes our own experience.

True to its chosen genre, Avalos walks a narrative tightrope between madness and the atavistic fear of the dead reawakening—is all that we see on the screen a genuine eruption of evil forces at work, or evidence of Rachel's slow spiral into insanity?—and he leads us by the hand to the end of that wire with assurance and skill. Though Avalos eschews graphic violence, there are a number of quiet but very real jolts (none more jarring than the first, which I won't betray here), but *Ghosts* is shaped above all by an exquisitely realized sense of being cast adrift in a consumptive, all-devouring environment that others seem to thrive upon, and the fearful realization that one might not escape intact—if at all. The steady slide from the inviting patio-parties and steamy hot tubs of sunny L.A., into the tangible malignancy of the avaricious rooms, homes, and streets is lovingly detailed by cinematographer/videographer Lukas Ettlin, whose work is cannily 'corrupted' by Scott Hale's palette of visual effects, in which flesh can quiver into rot with the subtle shift of an eyebrow or deepening of a shadow. Vincent Gillioz's score is the black icing on the cake, smooth, slippery, and insidious.

There are, to be sure, echoes of older genre works here, including almost-forgotten cinematic sleepers like *Let's Scare Jessica to Death* and *Eyes of Fire*. While the catalyst of *Ghosts* is venerable indeed—tales entangling possessive spirits, 'magick' and madness date back to the Hebrew 'dybbuk,' the contemporary template arguably established with Henry James' "The Turn of the Screw" and H.P. Lovecraft's "The Case of Charles Dexter Ward"—the fresh orientation Avalos brings to GHOSTS is deceptively pragmatic, easing into a parable that charts the black heart of the contemporary fringe-Hollywood scene.

As the couple settle into their new home, cozily sharing their creative work space with chair backs practically touching, the widening rift between them is defined in part by the deadening writer's block one suffers while the other savors a rush of productivity. Jealousy flares, fueling Rachel's growing distress and certainty that something is terribly amiss.

The steady tapping of the keyboard becomes as violative as the overt manifestations of demonic children, sentient woodwork, and fleeting specters, and the absurdity of the coveted muse ("channeling" a by-the-numbers script for a western as old as, well, Tom Mix) embodies *The Ghosts of Edendale*'s malignant forces at work. In stark contrast to the repetitive rant-manuscript of Jack Nicholson's aspiring author in Stanley Kubrick's *The Shining*, Kevin's script is—damn it!—praised and embraced by the unseen powers-that-be, optioned, and quickly opens doors that remain frustratingly out-of-reach to others... including Rachel.

Surely, the productive partner must be possessed: what else could explain the unnatural ability to create in a conceptual-ly-bankrupt, culturally-impoverished city where "properly-channeled" (read: recycled) creativity is the coin of the realm?

Whatever possesses Avalos and Connor and their partners in crime, let's hope we see more manifestations of their creative chemistry—and soon.

- Stephen R. Bissette

© 2003

That, by the way, is 905 words complete—I figured it was too long for the zine, but I have no problem re-writing, revising or editing material down to length. I used to struggle with that process (since you can't ask Chas any longer, just ask other editors

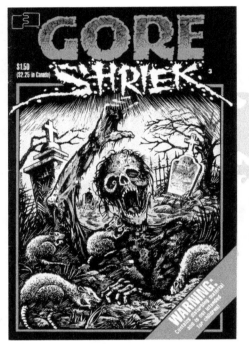

I've worked with and/or for, like Tim Lucas, Steve Murphy, or Mike Dobbs), but my two-plus years (1999–2001+) of writing a weekly video review column for local newspapers taught me the art of revision, compression and compromise, and to accept editorial cuts whenever necessary.

To that end, I also sent along (prior to receiving a reply) a shorter review, which clocks in at 481 words:

THE GHOSTS OF EDENDALE (2003)

The California Gold Rush never ended. Tales of dead 'old Los Angeles' spreading its clammy presence into 'new Los Angeles' are as old as the Hollywood hills. There's ghosts in them thar hills, feeding on irrational dreams of wealth, celebrity, and virtual immortality that draws generation after generation to fame or ignoble obscurity. Writer-director-editor Stefan Avalos (*The Money Game*, 1994; *The Last Broadcast*, 1998, co-directed by Lance Weiler) resurrects the archetype with the eerie, unsettling *The Ghosts of Edendale*. Set in his adopted L.A. neighborhood and filmed in his own home, Avalos and producer Marianne Connor (*Impressions of Jordan*, *Time 'til Light*) craft a chilling gem.

Kevin (Stephen Wastell of *The Money Game*, *The Miner's Massacre*) and Rachel (Paula Ficara) find their 'dream house' in

"Fuuuuccck. You know what I'm talking about, Bissette, after all we've been through. You've been in deeper trenches then I have; we've been there and back.

Shit, man!

Life is just too fucking short."

historic Edendale, bedrock of the movie capital, planning to write screenplays to build a new life far from a sketchy past back East. Kevin is intrigued by their new home's history and happy to find their neighbors (including Keith Fulton and Louis Pepe, makers of *The Hamster Factor and Other Tales of Twelve Monkeys* and *Lost in La Mancha*) also work in movies. Rachel, however, suffers 'second sight' of Edendale's underbelly, and her suffocating dread shapes the film.

True to its genre, *Ghosts* walks a tightrope between madness and fear of the dead reawakening—is all that we see truly evil forces at work, or Rachel's spiral into insanity?—with assurance and skill. Punctuated by quiet but very real jolts (none more jarring than the first), *Ghosts* evokes the horror of being cast adrift in a consumptive, all-devouring environment that others thrive upon. The steady slide from patio-parties and hot tubs into malignant, avaricious environments is detailed by cinematographer Lukas Ettlin, 'corrupted' by Scott Hale's visual effects (flesh quivers into rot with the shift of an eyebrow), and again, Vincent Gillioz's insidious score is black icing on the cake.

There are echoes of older genre works here (*Let's Scare Jessica to Death*, *Eyes of Fire*, *The Shining*); possessive spirits date back to the Hebrew 'dybbuk,' the contemporary template established with Henry James' "The Turn of the Screw" and Lovecraft's "The Case of Charles Dexter Ward." But Avalos' orientation is deceptively pragmatic, offering a parable of the fringe-Hollywood scene. These ghosts pitch Rachel's deadening writer's block against Kevin's rush of productivity. The tapping of the keyboard becomes as violative as the specters, and the absurdity of the coveted muse ("channeling" a by-the-numbers script for a western as old as, well, Tom Mix) embodies *Ghosts*'s malignant terrors. Surely, the productive partner must be possessed: what else could explain the unnatural ability to create in a city where "properly-channeled" (read: recycled) creativity is the coin of the realm?

Whatever possesses Avalos and Connor and their partners in crime, let's hope we see more manifestations of their creative chemistry—and soon.

- Stephen R. Bissette

© 2003

So, anyway, that was the first exchange.

Here's the initial follow-up response from the editor (edited only to remove identification):

From: -----------------

To: "'Marge & Steve Bissette'"

Subject: RE: Steve Bissette following up phone call w/review for GHOSTS

Date: Wed, 22 Oct 2003 12:35:59 -0400

Hi Steve!

No worries about the cold call. We don't usually accept them but in your case, we'll make an exception. ;) Thank you for the review. I've read it and it's quite good but far too long for our ----- section; the word count for reviews there is 350 words, unless it is a major, much-anticipated release. I understand if you don't want to cut your review down to a third of its size but unfortunately you'll have to if we run it in the mag. If you want to keep it intact and offer someone else the review that's totally fine, and submit something else (that's 350) to me in the future that would be great! I'd love to add you to our roster of freelancers. LOVE your artwork by the way... you are hugely talented. You don't happen to have any *Swamp Thing* art prints for sale do you? It would look great at the ------- mansion.

Not a bad start, I thought.

Stupid me.

I sent out a care package of my comics, all signed/personalized, and replied immediately, attaching a 345-word rewrite of my review:

Howdy, ------,

THANK YOU for the prompt reply, and thanks for excusing the 'cold call.' Didn't see how else to proceed, and glad I didn't offend.

Happy to revise the review to fit your needs, and save the long version for other uses. You open for that?

Also -- happy to interview [the filmmakers], IF you're interested. [I also suggested a related article and interview with a relevant filmmaker.] Just a thought.

I'd love to write for you folks -- and now that I've got both your name and address and ----'s, I'll grease the wheels a bit with some gift packs of comics and prints via snail mail. Hey, tis the season.

All the best, look forward to your reply,

Steve B

And here's the initial condensation and rewrite:

The Ghosts of Edendale (2003) haunt Hollywood's most venerable bedrock neighborhood. The malingering spirits of silent-movie 'days gone by' seep like waterstains from the walls and fences as Kevin (Stephen Wastell of *The Miner's Massacre*) and Rachel (Paula Ficara of *El Chupacabra*) move into their 'dream house' to build a new life (far from a sketchy past "back East") writing screenplays. The fissures in their cozy creative domesticity manifest with the titular ghosts: Kevin loves their new home, its history, and the odd neighbors who make movies, and immediately begins cranking out a saleable script. Rachel, alas, can't write a workable page and alone sees Edendale's underbelly as 'it' possesses hubby.

Set and filmed in his adopted L.A. neighborhood, this is writer/director Stefan Avalos's follow-up to the pioneer digital chiller *The Last Broadcast* (1998, co-directed by Lance Weiler). Extending the potential of the medium, Avalos and producer Marianne Connor craft a chilling gem that deservedly won the Silver Lake Award at the Silver Lake Film Festival in September, 2003; on the heels of its festival and theatrical play, MTI releases *Ghosts* on video/DVD in August. Echoing *Let's Scare Jessica to Death* (Rachel's suffocating dread shapes the film) and Lovecraft's "The Case of Charles Dexter Ward", *Ghosts* delineates the quiet horror of a consumptive, all-devouring environment. The insidious slide from patio-parties and hot tubs into madness is populated by fleetingly-glimpsed specters (none more startling than the first, erupting from a closet) and the quiver of flesh into rot with the lift of an eyebrow. Thus, *Ghosts* is a film of subtleties, sans bloodshed: not everyone's cup of tea, I know, but taken on its own understated terms it's a treat. As in *The Last Broadcast*, Avalos' orientation to the genre is deceptively pragmatic. In the end, *Ghosts* is a telling parable of the fringe-Hollywood scene. Surely, Kevin is possessed: what else could explain his churning out a vapid script so perfectly suited to contemporary Hollywood's impoverished creative marketplace? *Ghosts* is a fresh of fresh fetid air to all but the most ravenous gorehounds, and highly recommended.

What followed was a long stretch—weeks—of silence.

***

Part the Third—Being a Chronology of Some Woe, Concerning That Which Was Not Deemed Fit to "Entertain" or "Enlighten," and That Which Was, But Was Not Paid For, Thus Published to the Loss of Only the Author, Sweetened as it were with Some Flights of Pique and Passages of Moribund Musings, and Ending As Promised Without Proper Resolution, Save for the Usual Niggardly Dissolution.

So, after the long silence following the submission of my revised review of *The Ghosts of Edendale* (a wait I must admit I have inflicted on others, too, inadvertently, especially as an editor), I finally received a reply when I prompted one at last with more than one increasingly aggressive, but unfailingly polite, email.

The email from Ye Editor of Note that I received almost two months after submission of the revised text was rather condescending.

In short, it urged me to rewrite the review again—not for word count, which was fine, but because, well, I had liked the film too much, you see. Ye Editor (who had not seen the film, nor even heard of it until I'd brought it to their attention) pressed me for negative comments in the revision. "Isn't there some flaw, something that doesn't work in the film?" the editor pressed.

Ye Editor also expressed some concern that this was a film that wasn't yet in general distribution, or on video or DVD. Why write about it?

I was also given a pointed sentence or two on the magazine's preferred writing style, which was amusing because it was, for all intents and purposes, a distillation of my amigo Chas Balun's writing style.

Well, actually, I'm being too kind.

It was, if I may be so bold, actually a complete and generational appropriation and ransacking of Chas' once-original voice and style. The magazine not only absorbed and adopted Chas' manner of writing: the magazine had codified it, stolen it wholesale, made it "their own," and were proffering it as a style guide, essentially. Curse words were encouraged, critical barbs preferred. It was the matter-of-fact, no-shit, dick-in-the-dirt review style Chas had introduced and institutionalized for horror fandom with his seminal little self-published pamphlets *The Connoisseur's Guide to the Contemporary Horror Film* and *The Gore Score* back in the day, which Chas further indoctrinated as his own via *Deep Red* magazine.

Now, I had written for Chas and *Deep Red* many times; as I've said before and will till the day I die, it was Chas who first opened the door for me as a published writer, and *Deep Red* was the initial vehicle. I knew the style, and I knew the source.

I bit my tongue, though, as I didn't want to respond angrily, noting that I had been writing in "the magazine's preferred style" while its publisher, and Ye Editor, I was hoping to curry favor with were most likely still in grade school, or at best, junior high.

I instead wrote a polite letter asserting that (a) I knew their magazine well, and

"The Gore Score back in the day, which Chas further indoctrinated as his own via Deep Red magazine."

its preferred writing style, which was one I'd indeed indulged myself in the pages of *Deep Red*; (b) while I was certainly willing to do another rewrite—still on spec—I was writing about a film I was enthusiastic about, and didn't care to waste any portion of my 345 word count citing flaws that didn't seem worthy of mention and would be in fact contrary to the spirit, intent and content of my review and my reason for writing it; (c) it was worth writing about because it was a new work from a filmmaker of some significance, and I was deliberately submitting the review early so as to provide their magazine with a 'scoop,' and (d) in the spirit of cooperation and making it clear my intentions were pure, I offered a further review of a film I'd seen no one else write about anywhere. In fact, I sent two drafts of the review, one long, one short, as I had with *Ghosts of Edendale*.

Furthermore, I carefully selected a film that offered the kind of gore quotient most gorehounds prefer, and that incorporated negative comments among the positive comments, which seemed somehow essential to this editor. I also chose a film and review that appropriately incorporated the tenor, tone and slang typical of my *Deep Red* work.

I was now offering the editor two drafts of two spec reviews, of two films no other genre magazine had covered to date. This would seem to be an exclusive of sorts, though I didn't assert that aggressively as yet—I did, however, remind Ye Editor that I was able to contact both filmmakers, and would be happy to expand my reviews into full articles or interviews, if the magazine were at all interested.

Here's the reviews I offered in the spirit of freelancer peace, good will, and further cooperation, and in hopes of landing one or the other in the pages of their magazine. The second, shorter draft was also 'punched up' to fit Ye Editor's request for edgier writing:

THE CHAMPAGNE CLUB (2002; Dir/Scr: Joao Machado):

Michael Naismith once sang about "running from the Grand Ennui," but this handsomely mounted threnody plunges into the Grand Canyon of ennui. Direction, photography, art direction, music, and performances are fine and perfectly tuned with this upscale production's nihilistic descent into a self-made hell. It's a harrowing, graphic *Leaving Las Vegas* for the elite urban gallery set.

Joao Machado's debut feature bottles up a quartet of L.A.'s young art-scene nouveau rich in a remote tropical estate and lets them fester. Initially drawn together by their shared discomfort over the "pendulum swing between art and commerce" in which they owe their wealth & privilege to exploitation rather than creation, in due course (or, should I say, multiple courses, each more vile than the last) they destroy all the art in sight and willingly slide from boredom, narcissism, alienation and despair to self-degradation, self-mutilation, madness, coprophilia, cannibalism, and beyond.

When all is said and done (and eaten), this is arch and calculatedly gross fare, but there's no denying Machado chronicles ground-zero emotional auto-cannibalism with exquisite clarity. He also boasts impeccable credentials, both personal (the film is dedicated to his father, painter Juarez Machado, and mother, "consecrated grand culinary chef" Eliane Carvalho) and cinematic. Machado brazenly plunders thematics, dramaturgy, and specifics from a stellar pantheon of art-(charnel)house horrors: Luis Bunuel's *The Exterminating Angel*, Marco Ferreri's *La Grande Bouffe*, Pasolini's *Salo*, and Peter Greenaway's *The Cook, the Thief, His Wife and Her Lover*, amid resonant imagery echoing Kubrick's *The Shining* (Tim's hallway visions of butchering his companions), Argento's *Suspiria* (the final closeup of Connie in a pool of blood spreading on a decoratively tiled floor), the anarchic Brazilian master work *Macunaima* (the swimming pool 'soup'), and key works by painters like Rene Magritte and others.

Machado orchestrates this tapestry without compromising the integrity of his own vision; indeed, though he borrows much and acknowledges all his debts along the way, the potent framing device —opening and closing with perfect symmetry—succinctly anchors his conceits and keeps the film from becoming merely derivative navel-gazing. That much of it is risible (nude Bruce eating and humping his man-sized portion of mashed potatoes) allows one to keep watching, even while the gorge rises. Machado intends to provoke, disgust, and outrage, but amid the current art house wave of explicit grue and sex (dominated by French imports like *Baise Moi*, *See the Sea*, *Fat Girl*, and *Trouble Every Day* peppered with more domestic fare like *Titus* and *American Psycho*), *The Champagne Club* seems tamer than it intends to be; casual viewers may consider this mannered wallow in 'poor little rich kids' degradation and despair much ado about nothing, while gorehounds and exploitation buffs won't

wade through the aristocratic angst to get to the grue. It's nevertheless disturbing, an engaging first film; Machado is a filmmaker well worth following, a talent to watch.

———

THE CHAMPAGNE CLUB (2002; Dir/Scr: Joao Machado):

Joao Machado's debut feature locks a quartet of L.A.'s young art-scene nouveau rich into a remote tropical estate and watches 'em fester. Their snobby discomfort over the "pendulum swing between art and commerce"—they owe their wealth & privilege to exploitation rather than cre-

"It was Chas who first opened the door for me as a published writer, and Deep Red was the initial vehicle."

ation—prompts the slide from boredom, narcissism, alienation and despair dips into self-degradation, self-mutilation, madness, coprophilia, cannibalism, and beyond— [the title of the magazine I was submitting to] turf, no doubt.

When all is said, done, and eaten, this is gross shit, but Machado chronicles ground-zero emotional auto-cannibalism with exquisite clarity. Direction, photography, art direction, music, and performances are perfectly attuned to this upscale produc-

tion's nihilistic descent into self-made hell. Machado boasts impeccable credentials (the film is dedicated to his father, painter Juarez Machado, and mother, "consecrated grand culinary chef" Eliane Carvalho), and he plunders from a stellar pantheon of art-(charnel)house horrors: Luis Bunuel's *The Exterminating Angel*, Marco Ferreri's *La Grande Bouffe*, Pasolini's *Salo*, and Peter Greenaway's arty horrors. Still, there are echoes of Kubrick's *The Shining* (the hero's hallway visions of butchering his companions), Argento's *Suspiria* (the blood of one female victim spreads across a decoratively tiled floor), the anarchic 'lost' Brazilian masterpiece *Macunaima* (a swimming pool charnelhouse 'soup'), and references to painters like Rene Magritte.

Machado orchestrates this tapestry without compromising his vision; he borrows much and acknowledges all his debts, but the potent framing device—opening and closing with perfect symmetry—anchors the film and keeps it from becoming pretentious navel-gazing. Much of it is hilarious (one nude yuppie scarfs and humps a man-sized portion of mashed potatoes); Machado intends to provoke, disgust, and outrage, but amid the current art house wave of explicit grue and sex (dominated by French imports like *Baise Moi* and *Irreversible*), *The Champagne Club* seems tamer than it intends to be. Many will consider this mannered wallow in 'poor little rich kids' degradation much ado about nothing, gorehounds and exploitation buffs will be hard-pressed to stomach the snotty angst to reach the grue. Still, an engaging first film; keep an eye out for future Machado mayhem.

OK, that's the pair. A rewrite of my *Ghosts of Edendale* review was also attached, though the changes were minor and inconsequential.

This garnered a response.

Ye Editor liked this new review of this new film, which no one at the zine had ever heard of, and if I'd be willing to indulge their making a few editorial revisions, they would like to run it.

Those changes were so minor, they weren't going to give me the chance to make them myself. And, in fact, they were thinking about assigning a writer to interview the director of *The Champagne Club*.

Got that?

Assigning another writer to do an interview I'd proposed to do.

Fucking hell!

And still, no response on the initial review of *The Ghosts of Edendale*, which I'd now rewritten three times.

This is what is laughingly called, in most circles, "being professional."

Freelancers must always "be professional."

Now, an odd bit of banter followed. Note the dates of the following email exchanges.

From: "--------"

To: "'Marge & Steve Bissette'"

Subject: RE: Steve Bissette w/Slight rewrite on GHOSTS OF EDENDALE review, here --

Date: Sat, 21 Feb 2004 20:38:43 -0500

Steve, just a quick note to let you know that the director of *Champagne Club* asked for the text from the review and he was really happy with it, he plans to use quotes in the marketing of the movie. Cool!

Managing Editor, ---------------

Dear ----,

Good news, that. I've already been an asset to [your magazine] and the director; what more can one ask in this lifetime?

Stay in touch,

Best,

Steve B

That was sarcasm, falling on deaf ears.

What more can one ask?

How about getting a clear response to my initial submission, or not having something I turned the zine onto result in some other writer getting the assignment, particularly since I offered to interview the filmmaker already?

Of course, being paid for the review the editor just accepted would be nice, too.

But I'm getting ahead of myself a bit—the email exchanges continue, with a sudden right turn into Ye Editor encouraging me to get back into comics and indulging

anew in fresh diversionary flattery:

From: "--------"

To: "'Marge & Steve Bissette'"

Subject: RE: Steve Bissette w/Slight rewrite on GHOSTS OF EDENDALE review, here --

"The magazine not only absorbed and adopted Chas' manner of writing: the magazine had codified it, stolen it wholesale, made it 'their own.'"

Date: Sun, 22 Feb 2004 17:54:44 -0500

That and you're a WICKEDLY talented artist. I loved your Swamp Thing years and collected Taboo religiously. You're also an accomplished writer, it's an honour to have you on board. Keep at the comics though, Mignola was lucky, if Guillermo wasn't such a Hellboy fan, that film would never have been made (it took GDT 6 years to get it going), so it takes just one determined person to really like your stuff! And everyone likes your stuff...

-------, Managing Editor

Dear ------,

Too late—I retired from comics in 1999. So it goes...

I've kept myself productive, though. Amid writing for *Video Watchdog* now and again and the occasional review (such as those you now have in hand), I illustrate at least one novel/anthology a year to keep my hand in the ink. Also, working on a book-length study of Vermont and New England films, and just wrapping up the first issue of my own regional film zine, *Green Mountain Cinema*. Also starting work-in-earnest this week on a planned feature-length video production adapting my good friend and folklorist Joe Citro's *Vermont Ghost Guide* for release the end of this coming Fall. We're shooting in June, if all goes well. Wish us luck.

But comics? It's history, for me. 24 years was a good career, but the industry just got too fucking sour by the end. After the direct sales market collapsed and my divorce nailed me, I decided I'd had a good run, and have moved on with nary a look back.

But thanks for the very kind words.

All the best,

Steve B

From: "---------"

To: "'Marge & Steve Bissette'"

Subject: RE: Back to you, from Steve B...

Date: Mon, 23 Feb 2004 12:17:29 -0500

Understood. I am in the middle of a divorce myself, wouldn't wish it upon my worst enemy.

Oh, forgot to mention *Gore Shriek*, that was a blast too.

---------, Managing Editor

At this point, I was beyond pissed.

This was getting amusing.

I mean, how long could this go on? What would this process stretch out to? How unprofessional could this get, over a single submission?

I decided to find out.

Tired of these pleasantries I ventured the leap: since my review of *The Champagne Club* was accepted, what, please, were their payment rates? Copyright remains mine, yes? Is there a contract or letter of agreement Ye Editor could offer, detailing the terms of our arrangement?

From: "----------"

To: "'Marge & Steve Bissette'"

Subject: RE: Hello from Steve B, re: GHOSTS OF EDENDALE, and review matters...

Date: Mon, 23 Feb 2004 13:01:51 -0500

As for our rates, they're low already because we are an independently published magazine, ...so don't expect to retire on submissions [to our zine]! ;) Please ask ----- [email address contact followed] for a final word count for your submission, then submit an invoice to her.

Thanks!

-------, Managing Editor

Dear -----,

OK, good start. More details, please.

Let me wait for your decision on *Ghosts*—that is, after all, the film I really wanted to cover, if you'll have me and it—and then we'll work out something.

Thanks, all the best,

Steve B

I also pressed Ye Editor to provide me the final word count of their revised edit, which I was not privy to; when I contacted the contact Ye Editor had steered me to, I was told to submit my word count and invoice.

I did so, using my own final word count, and—nothing happened.

Come the month of April—remember, this process started in October of the year before—I wrote the following to Ye Editor, ccing it to Ye Publisher, too:

From: Marge & Steve Bissette

Sent: Tuesday, April 13, 2004 10:04 AM

To: ---------

Cc: ----------

Subject: Hello from Steve Bissette -- GHOSTS OF EDENDALE review??

Dear ----------,

Hope this finds you and yours well, and that you had a fine Easter.

A recent visit to the newsstand allowed me to purchase a copy of the new ----------- with my [*Champaign Club*] review. Handsome cover, indeed!

Any decision at all on the rewrite I submitted of the *Ghosts of Edendale* review? Payment for the review you've now published? Please advise.

Best,

Steve Bissette

From: "-------------"

"Shit, Bissette, you'd think our having so many years under our belts would mean something," Chas said at one point. "All I'm tasting is shit in my mouth!"

To: "'Marge & Steve Bissette'"

Subject: RE: Hello from Steve Bissette -- GHOSTS OF EDENDALE review??

Date: Wed, 21 Apr 2004 16:00:37 -0400

Steve! Don't buy ---------! We would have sent you a copy, you contributed!

Sorry it took me so long to get back to you, I've been away a lot and changed our cover story last minute last issue so it's been crazy. Unfortunately I didn't run the *Ghosts* review, (it's not the writ-

ing by the way!) [The publisher] just keeps cutting all the indie stuff from ---------, there is always the --------- section but I have a feeling it's too late by now...

Seen anything interesting lately? I really want to see *Shaun of the Dead*! That looks hilarious. Where are you based out of by the way?

------------, Managing Editor

Dear --------,

Ah, just back from vacation.

I'd welcome copies of --------- with my review; still, did buy a couple. My mailing address:

Stephen R. Bissette

USA

(Meaning, 'natch, I'm based in Vermont!)

In lieu of payment, how about a -------- subscription? Let me know -- even if it's only comp copies for four issues, that would be fine with me.

Just heard via the video grapevine (I work in video retail in part, remember) that *Ghosts of Edendale* is coming out from WARNER (!!!) in the fall. Great news, that, since it means a good little indy will enjoy wider distribution via a major label... though I doubt it'll add up to more money for the filmmakers, knowing how these studios operate.

I've stepped away from my day-job and am re-engaging with creative life, enjoying enough of a financial cushion (thanks to an unexpected legal job AND the windfall royalties on the JOHN CONSTANTINE film—remember, I co-created that character in *Swamp Thing*).

...Should be a busy spring, summer and fall, so don't fret if I don't send more reviews your way. But do, please, wish me luck.

And do, please, run the *Ghosts* review at SOME point. You've got a SCOOP, damn it!!!

All the best, stay in touch,

Steve B

From: "------------"

To: "'Marge & Steve Bissette'"

Subject: RE: Hello from Steve Bissette -- GHOSTS OF EDENDALE review??

Date: Thu, 29 Apr 2004 10:02:13 -0400

Steve!

Wow this is all great news! And of course I know you co-created *Constantine*, what do you think I am, an amateur??? ;) I've been a comic junkie my whole life and have been reading both *Swamp Thing* and *Hellblazer* for ages. You're hugely talented dude, your 80's run with Moore and Totleben on *Swamp Thing* was by far the best. Guess you don't happen to have any old pencils kicking around for sale after two decades do you? *wishful thinking* Love that fucking art!

Have you read Andy Diggle's new take on *Swamp Thing* it yet? Did you see the *Constantine* film yet? Keanu Reeves? *shudder* and why the hell does it take place in L.A.?? WTF?? Hollywood.

I also read *Taboo* by the way. Small world huh?

Yes we can do a swap, I'll put you on the comp list for a year. Sound good? (I'm not surprised you're in Vermont either)

Dude, keep me updated on... [projects]!

And I will run that review, especially if they've been picked up by Warner. You are right, they'll likely get hosed by the studio but at least people will see their movie!

Congrats on flexing your creative muscles again... You rock Steve!

------------, Managing Editor

My mid-May reply:

Hello, ---------,

Apologies for the slow reply, I'm JUST home from two weeks of travel. The second week was spent on a video industry seminar/conference/retreat; among the tidbits gleaned there was the news that *Ghosts of Edendale* is indeed on WARNER BROS. slate for Halloween release. Include THAT in the review, please! It's now a fact, or at least a factoid.

...What's your deadline for the OCTOBER issue of ---------? I'll make sure you get all the info/contacts you need in time for that deadline...

No on seeing *Constantine*—though it has to be better than *Van Helsing*—and I don't imagine I'll be invited to the NYC premiere, either, but you never know. Will keep you posted. Agreed on the casting... but, what the hell. It's out of our hands!

And THANK YOU for accepting the barter agreement. I'd love a -------- sub, and happy to keep the occasional review or text piece coming your way to keep the subscription current and active.

More later, all the best,

Steve B

Well, to cut to the chase, I never got my comp copies of the issue of the zine my review of *The Champaign Club* appeared in—a movie that, to date, has never gained release theatrically or on video.

The film that did get wide DVD release was (natch) *The Ghosts of Edendale*, but outside of video industry magazine trade reviews, *The Ghosts of Edendale* was

> "*I know you co-created Constantine, what do you think I am, an amateur??? ;)*"

completely ignored by genre journalists and magazines. The film, and its makers, deserved better. To the best of my knowledge, my review never ran, though I'd submitted it to Ye Editor a full year before the film's Warner DVD release.

I'm not sure whether or not my review ever ran because I never got the promised subscription in payment for the review of mine they published.

Needless to say, I ceased submitting to this particular editor, and ceased buying their magazine with any regularity.

I wish I could say this was unusual, but it's pretty typical of the magazine publishing world. There have been similar experiences, but I've offered this particular case history because it is far, far more entertaining than most. Nobody got hurt, and however insulting it proved to be, its documentation is highly hilarious. In the end, my

telling of it in some detail at least promotes two good films by two young filmmakers worthy of attention.

See, some good might come of it all.

Alas, things did not go so well for many of my friends, associates, and peers who "hung in there" with magazines like *Rue Morgue*—or, back to basics, the very publisher and magazine Chas and I had once freelanced for, *Fangoria*. Remember Josh Hadley, who wrote the *Fangoria* column about horror movies only viewable on VHS? Josh writes:

"I had heard about non-payment issues with the previous ownership of *Fangoria* (back when they were a Starlog publication), but I was always paid on time under Alexander's reign on the magazine. I did catch little bits here and there of some troubles, and a few times the magazine was delayed in printing, but I was assured it was all okay and again, I was paid on time so I figured it was all good in the end. Only looking back does the scuttlebutt fall into the larger context.

Then Alexander left and Michael Gingold was given the big chair. That didn't go over well as he very publicly left the magazine (of which he had been part since the late 1980s) under less than desirable circumstances.[11] My payments stopped around this time although my work continued to be published. The issues stopped being printed and began appearing as 'digital only' issues shortly thereafter. I was assured I would get paid, though—the magazine was okay, they just needed to get some more ad revenue and then they could print the issues and everything would be fine. Then the delays got longer and longer and longer until what was meant as the saving grace Hail Mary play that was the Kevin Smith edited issue... it seems that this was a make it or break it issue and it did not make it. Keep in mind the magazine had been digital only for four issues now and subscribers were getting pissed off. All the while, announcements of 'printing next

11 See Steve Barton, "Michael Gingold Leaves Fangoria," Dread Central, May 24, 2016, archived online at http://www.dreadcentral.com/news/167956/michael-gingold-leaves-fangoria/ , and Graham Winfrey, "Fangoria Editor-in-Chief Michael Gingold Fired After 28 Years – Guillermo del Toro and Others Offer Support," *IndieWire*, June 1, 2016, archived online at http://www.indiewire.com/2016/06/fangoria-fires-editor-in-chief-michael-gingold-guillermo-del-toro-28-years-horror-magazine-1201682340/

week' kept coming at a regular basis on the *Fangoria* website and Twitter feed and Facebook page. Ad rates were subsequently cut in half…it was unlikely the issues would ever see print. I was told over and over again in this period to just hang on a little longer and I would get my back pay— just a little longer. I liked my editor at the time, so I gave him the benefit of the doubt."

After limping as far into the 21st century as it could gimp, *Fangoria* came to a dismal end at last.

It was an end Chas did not live to see, but that left many freelancers I know (and more that I don't know) impoverished, ripped-off, and feeling about the horror "journalism" industry pretty much the way Chas did in his final years.

Like most monster and horror movies, though, "the end" was not the end, really. Josh continues:

"As it stands now, I have not been paid in over a year, I am owed a four-digit amount and I am sure others are, as well. From what I can tell, owner Tom Defeo is still living in his large house and I guarantee that Kevin Smith got paid for his issue—yet the people who made that issue are not. I have spoken to a few of the other writers and artists and none of them have been paid either. They mostly have accepted that It's done and they are not getting paid. I am not. We did the work, the work was printed and we deserve payment. Some of them are afraid of making a public stink fearing that it will paint them as troublemakers and costing them future jobs."

I myself donated (as a gift) $150 US to Josh Hadley after he'd been stiffed by *Fangoria*, to help cover the legal costs of filing suit in his home state's small claims court in hopes of finally being paid, and he was owed for freelance work that had been commissioned and published before the magazine folded.

"I will not let Defeo get away with this. I sued Defeo and even won a judgment[12]—but I am unable to collect. See,

since I sued him from Wisconsin (where I am located) and he is in New York, neither state will enforce a judgment from the other. If I want to see my money I have to re-sue him in NY court and there I have to pay, all over again, and I have

"Some of them are afraid of making a public stink fearing that it will paint them as troublemakers…"

to be present in court. This is not feasible so… Defeo gets away with ripping me and everyone else off. …The man knows what he did: he actively dodged my process servers, they told me they saw lights go out when they approached his home…. Funny though: after I sued him and since I continue to go after him and *Fangoria* in public. I have been blocked from their Twitter and Facebook feeds. These are not people who are in a tough

spot, they know exactly who they are.

I was told, again and again in good faith, that payment was coming and just hang in a little longer. My editor was genuinely someone I think was doing the best he could to save a sinking ship while its captain (Defeo) was…at the helm. I wanted to help Ken (Hanley) out, so I left it alone. Once, I found out that Defeo was ready to actually file bankruptcy I decided I had to say something. He does not deserve to get away clean with this."[13]

Ya, I know. This shit can really get you down. To many, this is all moot, since most online "publications" from **Huffington Post**[14] on down don't pay their writers anyway. "Who cares?" is posited by some as a rational point of view.

Remember, though: Chas didn't change everything by writing for *Fangoria*, or any newsstand magazine.

12 Josh indeed won this judgment: see the Wisconsin Court System Circuit Court Access, "Josh Hadley vs. Thomas Defeo," Door County Case Number 2017SC000010, filing date 01-09-2017, archived online at https://wcca.wicourts.gov/caseDetails.do;jsessionid=3E9F7B3BAFD-FEA1E1EA1FB27FFFB5DB7.render6?case-No=2017SC000010&countyNo=15&cacheId=B-C00648A74F0ABBA85F17A28E03E1392&re-cordCount=14&offset=0

13 Josh Hadley, November 5th, 2017 email to the author; quoted with permission. I asked Josh to offer his account of this sorry chapter in *Fangoria*'s history, as fellow freelancers need to know. *Fango*, you should have honored and paid your contributors.
14 Do they, or don't they? See Brendan James, "Unpaid Huffington Post Bloggers Actually Do Want to Get Paid," *International Business Times*, February 18, 2016, archived online at http://www.ibtimes.com/unpaid-huffington-post-bloggers-actually-do-want-get-paid-2313744

They came to him—after he'd self-published two nifty little 32-page softcover chapbooks, *The Connoisseur's Guide to the Contemporary Horror Film* (1983) and *The Gore Score* (1984) and peddled 'em for just $3.95 each.

Subsequently, a productive relationship with Tom Skulan at FantaCo Enterprises—first as a retailer/distributor, then as a publishing partner—spread the love, for as long as that lasted. They had a good run together, but Chas never found another Tom or FantaCo afterwards; as Chas used to say, "all things must pass."

Sometime after Chas had invited me into the tent to write for *Deep Red*, I had a hand in convincing another amigo who was getting fed up with the impoverishing frustrations of freelancing for genre magazines to consider self-publishing. That was my good friend Tim Lucas, and Tim and his wife, Donna Lucas, launched their self-published *Video Watchdog*, which also changed everything. Tim and Donna self-published 184 issues from 1990–2017, plus *VW* specials and a couple of books; they had a great run.

In very different ways, with very different critical visions and voices, Chas and Pat, Tim and Donna changed everything for the better (and not just in zines: the entire DVD and Blu-ray genre marketplace was transformed by what Chas and Tim brought to the table).

The moral?

I didn't say there was a moral—remember?

I could say DIY is best, and blow the self-publishing trumpet (hell, I'm back at it, and I'm in my 60s!), but for some creators and authors and artists and musicians, mutually beneficial rewards have been reaped via solid trustworthy relations with publishers and editors. In comics, I think of the Hernandez Brothers and *Love and Rockets* at Fantagraphics Publishing, Mike Mignola and *Hellboy* at Dark Horse Comics; there are similar success stories

"Flattery gets you nowhere, but magazine editors will get you nowhere a hell of a lot faster."

in every field, but they -are rare indeed—and those enjoying that kind of bond and productive longevity are rarer still.

I'd feel pangs of envy, but I've never even come close to tasting anything remotely like that in my lifetime. No sense crying over what you didn't and can't have. You work with the opportunities you can create, or that present themselves, and you make the most of 'em while they last.

Chas always did, and I always have, too.

Well, then: a moral?

OK, here ya go—and this got a good laugh out of Chas one afternoon in 2004 as I related the details of the above dance with *Rue Morgue* to him, via telephone:

Flattery gets you nowhere, but magazine editors will get you nowhere a hell of a lot faster.

[All the events depicted herein are true, and the email excerpts are actual excerpts from material in the SpiderBaby Archives. All names and specific references to those involved have been deleted to protect the guilty, though damned if I know why.][15]

15 Parts the Second and Parts the Third of this essay have been revised and expanded from a serialized article originally published on *Myrant,* December 10-11, 2005:
http://srbissette.blogspot.com/2005_12_10_archive.html
http://srbissette.blogspot.com/2005_12_11_archive.html
The comments are worth reading, including, "Having worked in the magazine industry for several years, I can't tell you how true this rings. Thanks for posting!"
As to the rest: As Chas would have said, "Ah, fuck it, Bissette! You hill-people are just *too* nice!" The magazine was *Rue Morgue,* the editor was Jovanka Vuckovic; I got news on December 9, 2009 that Jovanka had been replaced by Dave Alexander, and I went public with the news and the name of the magazine and editor involved the very next day. See the *Myrant* post for December 10, 2009—five years to the day after this essay was first posted on the original *Myrant* blog!—at: http://srbissette.com/?p=7401 …and no. I never got an apology, I never received the promised comp copies or subscription, and to ice this arsenic cake, about a year ago an issue of *Rue Morgue* with a cover story about the current *Swamp Thing* comic books used one of my 1980s DC Comics *Swamp Thing* covers—which I'd designed, penciled, and inked for DC—as that issue's *Rue Morgue* cover, sans credit, compensation, or even a 'thank you.' I don't care who is "in charge" at *Rue Morgue*: they've only added exploitative insult to past injury. The door is still open, *Rue Morgue,* if anyone at the helm cares to try to make things… you know, *nice.*

ADDENDUM:

Since the writing of this piece, two things have happened I must note:

(1) The great Dallas Mayr passed away on January 24, 2018, at age 71. Like Chas, Dallas had been battling cancer for a long while; words fail me. Those of us who were fortunate enough to know Dallas are still devastated, and the loss is still raw.

(2) As of late February 2018, the situation with Fangoria has dramatically changed.

A notice signed by Dallas Sonnier, Phil Nobile Jr., and "The New Blood at Fangoria" was posted online, and it read in part:

"Let's address the giant elephant in the room. So many of you bought and paid for subscriptions from Fangoria's previous publisher, but never received your order. Cinestate, Fangoria's new owner, had nothing to do with that…" but the notice goes on to promise the new publisher offers "a complimentary one-year subscription of the upcoming deluxe quarterly" to those who paid but were stiffed. More to the point of this Deep Red article:

"While the previous owner remains liable for all debts prior to us taking over a few days ago, we take your comments very seriously, and we are dedicated to doing whatever we can to make things right."

On February 16, 2018, Josh Hadley wrote me to say, "The new owner has been in contact and made good on all past issues so I am looking forward to Fangoria moving into the future."

As do we all at Deep Red.

My only cautionary note, to the former contributors and to the new management at Fangoria and GoreZone: some of us—yours truly included—never signed away any rights to our work for the previous publisher. I retain and own all copyrights to my published work in both publications, and the trademark to my GoreZone column. Please remember my former contributions are not among the assets, whatever those may be, that were purchased.

Best of luck, and thanks for the update, Josh!

BURBANK'S BLOODY BOOKSTORE

Photos: Greg Goodsell

An interview with Dark Delicacies' Del Howison

Kris Gilpin

I've known Del Howison for decades. Actor, writer, literary editor, and—along with his wife Sue—Del is the owner of Dark Delicacies, the only bookstore in the United States dedicated solely to horror literature and accessories. It was great when I lived in Burbank (the least pretentious area of L.A.) and was able to haunt the place regularly.

Now in its third incarnation, Dark Delicacies is still going strong. Chock-full of books and magazines, the store also stocks a vast array of DVDs, Blu-rays, posters, and other collectibles. Let's take a walk inside, have a talk with Del, and see what he has to say about his 20-plus years in the business…

DEEP RED: *I remember the tall, cool Frankenstein's Monster that was always outside your store…*

DEL HOWISON: [That was at] our second location. We had a seven-foot Frankenstein that stood out in front of the window on the sidewalk. A friend of mine named Tony built this platform that had small wheels on the back of it. There was a rough framework of what amounted to nothing more than a stickman. Tony got a T-shirt, a pair of pants, and a sport coat and dressed the frame. Then, every year after Halloween, I would go online to some costume site and buy whatever full-headed Frankenstein mask they had on sale. Every year, he had a different head. We would stuff it with newspapers and different shit we had laying around, and put it on top of the clothes. Then, in the back of the neck on the wooden frame, Tony attached a handle. When we wanted to roll Frankie out, we just grabbed the handle, tipped him up, and moved him like a two-wheeled cart. At the end of the day, we just reversed the process and brought him in. Now, the city of Burbank has some weird property lines. As it turned out, there was a space that belonged to the store on the front sidewalk—the city couldn't do anything about Frankie.

RED: *He was always so impressive standing there keeping guard. I was always afraid he'd get stolen. Whatever happened to him?*

DH: Well, when we moved to our current location, we owned no sidewalk. We couldn't take him with us. But, my customers had grown fond of him. One day, Frankie disappeared.

RED: *[Laughs] That's terrible!*

DH: There were reports of him in somebody's front yard two blocks away. Then, I'd hear of him being down the street. Seems Frankie went for a walk when he discovered he couldn't move with us!

"We had a seven-foot Frankenstein that stood out in front of the window on the sidewalk."

[Laughs] One of the last reports I received was that he was in North Hollywood at the warehouse of the Coffin Case guitar case company run by Jonny Coffin. If you ask me, I think Frankie and the Travelocity Gnome went off on retirement to someplace exotic.

RED: *How did you first become interested in horror in the first place?*

DH: Two things, really. I was the son of a Detroit cop, and lived through the riots of the '60s. Detroit has always been a city caught in an ebb and flow—a living thing following a long, straight line of building, destroying, and rebuilding. How it affects you really has a lot to do with your placement on that line. My position was always very close to the stuff of horror—both real and imagined. My parents were also members of a pretty strait-laced church of the Free Methodist persuasion. No dancing, no movies, no jewelry—blah, blah, blah. Very powerful stuff at a young age. Very controlling. It's very strange to look back on it as an adult to see how controlling it actually was.

RED: *Can you elaborate?*

DH: Sunday was a day of worship and rest. The last thing I was supposed to do was go outside after church and play. How profane is that? What an insult to God, this "children having fun" stuff! It wasn't a fire and brimstone kind of church like the neighboring Baptists, but the message they wanted you to know got through quite well. I found it all a bit confusing.

RED: *That's understandable…*

DH: It took most of my formative years to figure it out, and many decades after that to escape the guilt of the backsliders. You

don't realize how very cultish it is until you are able to step away far enough to get a good perspective on it.

RED: *Let's sidestep for a minute. You started out as an actor, and now have 26 acting credits to your name…*

DH: I've always said that I've mostly acted in "D" movies, but have occasionally been lucky enough for a "C" or "B" film. I started in theater—community, dinner, resort—all of them.

RED: *What was that like?*

DH: It was work, hard work. Anybody tells you differently, they weren't doing it right. I believe it was author Pat Conroy who said something like, "When you think you've gone deep enough, you haven't even scratched the surface." Once I moved to Los Angeles, some friends from Michigan were kind enough to let me crash at their place until I got my feet on the ground. I did some equity waiver and things, but was never able to get away from working full time to kickstart the acting. So, I sort of let it go. Funny thing was that once my wife and I opened Dark Delicacies, I received more acting offers than when I was kicking the streets trying to find work.

RED: *What can you tell me about acting in Bring Me the Head of Lance Henriksen? That's a great title, by the way.*

DH: Bring Me the Head of Lance Henriksen was shot by Michael Worth, and was all improv—sort of stream of consciousness, from what I could tell. There are a lot of good people it in who did scenes.

RED: *Such as?*

DH: Martin Kove, Adrienne Barbeau, John Saxon, and Cerina Vincent [were in it], but I'm not sure it was ever finished. It seems to have been in post-production hell for quite some time. The plot is loosely that Tim Thomerson is feeling over-the-hill as an actor and just isn't getting the amount of work that he'd like to be getting. Yet his friend Lance is working a lot. So… he becomes jealous and…whatever.

RED: *[Laughs…]*

DH: It was shot in a realistic documentary style. Anyway, we were holding a signing for something that involved Lance at Dark Delicacies one night, and Michael came into the store with Tim to shoot an improv scene or two. Michael grabbed a stack of laserdiscs that had a bunch of Trancers films in them. In this stack of discs, Michael put in a ringer—a film that Tim wasn't in. He asked me to play an autograph seeker. All Tim knew was that when Michael said, "Action!" we were rolling, but he didn't know what to expect. Like I said it, was all improv and adlib. So, the scene started. I walked up to Tim and said, "Mr. Thomerson would you please sign these discs for me?" He said, "Sure!" and started going through the small stack. At about the fourth disc was the ringer. "Sorry," he said. "I'm not in this one." I asked him, "Are you sure?" We went back and forth a couple of times until I snatched it back from him and said something like, "No wonder you're not popular anymore!" He was so smooth and so used to the style Michael Worth was shooting in that we were out in the one take with no problems. I hope the film comes out just for the fun of all the cameos.

"Bring Me the Head of Lance Henriksen was shot by Michael Worth."

RED: You started out as an extra in Clive Barker's Lord of Illusions.

DH: It was sheer luck that I was in the movie at all. Sue and I wanted to check out the filming of it, and there was a cattle call for extras. They needed to fill the Pantages Theater in Hollywood—it was where they were filming the big magic act scene with Kevin J. O'Connor.

RED: What was it like working with Clive Barker?

DH: Well, when we arrived, we were given a slip with a number on it. In order to help make the audience hang in there, they said that at some point during a break that Clive was going to select a number. That person would be brought up on stage to receive a gift. So, when the time came, Clive drew a number. It happened to be mine.

RED: Wow!

DH: I went up and got to stand next to him. My gift was to be in a scene they were going to shoot at the Magic Castle [a posh nightclub in Los Angeles—ed.].

RED: OK...

DH: The Magic Castle scene was at the bar. I distinctly remember Clive telling me, "All you have to do is sit at the bar with this lovely lady next to you like you're a customer. Drink beer and watch this magician perform hand magic with a coin." [Laughs] I was typecast in my first part. From that experience, Clive and I became good friends. He's been a big vocal supporter of Dark Delicacies from its very beginning. He's a very loyal person, and has signed at the store several times. I would do anything for him. An even bigger thrill for me was meeting both of his parents at an art exhibit he has down in Laguna Beach and taking a photo of the three of them together standing in front of his painting "The Arsonist".

RED: Moving on—you've played Dracula's Renfield character more than any other actor.

DH: I was really surprised when Video Watchdog editor Tim Lucas mentioned that in an article.

RED: How was it playing him four times for director Donald F. Glut?

DH: That's a lot of bug eating! Playing the character for Don was really interesting, since he let me approach it any way I wanted to. I didn't want to be crazy like Dwight Frye, since I thought Dracula would have demanded more out of his servant. It's not like he wanted to draw attention to himself. So, I played him as somebody who was fairly well-grounded except for a couple of eccentricities.

RED: What are some of your favorite acting experiences?

DH: Well, I love working in films with naked women for two reasons. First, I realize that if we're in a scene together, nobody in the audience is looking at me. Secondly, if I'm in a scene that is book-ended by two female nude scenes, you may as well change the name of my character to Fast Forward.

RED: You've also co-directed three horror projects. Was that fun for you?

DH: I love directing. I did some dinner theater directing prior to working in film. The major difference between directing stage and film is that on stage you get to move the actors about in a meaningful way to help tell and enhance the story. In film, you move the actors and the audience.

RED: Can you tell us some stories about the late Chas Balun?

DH: Chas was this big tall hippie kind of guy who had one of the easiest-going attitudes of anybody in the business. You would never take him for a splatter freak, or as he put it, a "chunkblowing enthusiast." But if you ever got him wound up, his excitement was palpable. He knew everything there was to know about splatter films, and in my opinion, put director Lucio Fulci on the radar. He signed at Dark Delicacies a few times, most notably for his books More Gore Score and Beyond Horror Holocaust. We would laugh like fools when we got together—his humor had no censorship. We appeared in a series of Dark Dreamer interviews for journalist and horror aficionado, Stanley Wiater. These were originally shot for, I believe, ON TV in Canada from about 1998 to 2001.

RED: What was the show like?

DH: It was a half-hour show [that consisted of either] a single interview with one person, or two 15-minute interviews put together for one episode. In 2011, Stanley put out a four-disc set containing most, if not all, of those interviews. One half-hour consisted of two interviews featuring Chas in one, and myself in the other. After author Richard Laymon died, we held a memorial gathering at Dark Delicacies and showed the episode featuring him as a tribute.

RED: Do you have any memories of Richard Laymon that you'd like to share?

DH: Dick was a good friend, and we loved joking around together. Back then, his young daughter, Kelly, would come with him and Ann to every horror convention. So, I met her in 1994 and we've been friends ever since. Dick liked coming to Dark Delicacies so much that for years whenever Kelly visited the store she would "bring" her dad with her—the wooden box containing his cremated remains—so that he wouldn't miss anything. Kelly and he were always welcome.

RED: You've edited many great award-winning horror anthologies. How did you and Jeff Gelb get the idea to edit the first Dark Delicacies book?

DH: Jeff put out a call for stories for book #12 in the erotic horror "Hot Blood" series, Strange Bedfellows, which was edited by himself and Michael Garrett. I submitted a tale called The Lost Herd. He bought it. When the book came out, we did a signing for it at Dark Delicacies. I talked with Jeff about the idea of doing an anthology series named after the store. The name was getting out there at that time. He could use the idea, and I could use his expertise in putting together an anthology. I learned on the job and learned from him. When we signed our first book contract together, we signed it on a morgue gurney that I happened to have in the store at the time.

RED: Really?

DH: It was the old porcelain type with the gutter all the way around and the drain with the silver screen in it. I use it to gross people out because you could still find hair dried to the drain screen. Richard Matheson wrote the introduction for the book of original tales, which included such authors as Clive Barker, Ramsey Campbell, John Farris, William F. Nolan, Richard Laymon, Whitley Strieber, F. Paul Wilson, Brian Lumley, Nancy Holder, Steve Niles, Joe R. Lansdale, and Chelsea Quinn Yarbro.

RED: How did you manage to snag Ray Bradbury?

DH: I knew Ray Bradbury as an acquaintance and wanted to get a story from him. He went through his files of unpublished short stories, and found what I think might be his only zombie story. He sent it to me to see if I liked it. I did. It was typical Ray Bradbury, with that golden haze of nostalgia to it, and yet a zombie story! He asked if he could update it a little and fiddle with it. He did, and when he was finished, we put in the book as the opening tale. It was the best $500 I could have spent for an original Bradbury. We won the Bram Stoker Award that year for Best Horror Anthology.

RED: How did you and Sue get the idea to start an all-horror store in the first place?

DH: We talked about it together, and kind of came up with the idea together. We did selling-tables at a couple of early conventions to see how things worked. One day in 1994, I came home and said to Sue, "I've got your store." We rented a storefront about three blocks from our house, and opened it with $5000 my mother had saved up for me, and by selling off our own collection. Sue would sell a book from her collection and then go in the back room and cry. But it all worked out. One of the coolest

"We've had Roger Corman, Clive Barker, Ernest Borgnine, James Wan, all the Jasons, and most of the Michael Meyers at one point or another."

things was that a friend of ours, Jay Patton, was moving the location of his bookstore in Phoenix and getting new shelving. One day, we were in our store painting the walls or something—getting it ready—when Jay walked in. He said, "I brought you my old bookshelves." He unloaded his van, and made a big pile of bookshelves in the middle of the store. Then, he was, "Gotta go!" He climbed back in his van, and drove back to Phoenix. Eight hours of driving, just to drop off his old bookshelves so we would have a better start. Across the board, if it hadn't been for friends, Dark Delicacies never would have happened. It's crazy good to have good friends.

RED: Did you ever have any anti-horror goons give you shit about your store?

DH: Not really. One time, this lady walked in, and Sue was behind the counter. These bas-reliefs of the art from of old tombstones (with skeletons and shit on them) were hanging on the wall. The lady asked Sue why she had them up there. Sue explained what they were, and added that they were just skeletons—we all have them inside us. The lady looked at her and said, "Yes, but do we need to be reminded?"

RED: Can you tell us a little about how the book signings at Dark Delicacies started out?

DH: We got the idea from attending the book signings at a great bookstore called

Dangerous Visions.

RED: How often do you hold them?

DH: When we started, we had one signing in the first month. Our first signer was Sara Karloff, Boris Karloff's daughter. From there, we never looked back. Nowadays, it isn't unusual to have eight to ten signing events a month.

RED: One of my favorite horror writers is Jack Ketchum, who recently passed away. Do you have any stories about him?

DH: The first time I had Ketchum, he said that he would come out if we flew him in. It was tight, but we felt it was worth it. When he arrived, he had his hand in a splint. I believe he had sprained it. Needless to say, he couldn't sign with it. I don't remember if he signed with his left hand or what, but somehow, we got through it. But, he was a great guy. We couldn't afford a fancy hotel room for him, so we used this tourist motel over by the Warner Brothers studio. The room had painted cinder block walls on the inside. Fancy, right? That place is still there, and overpriced because of location. We still refer to it as the "Ketchum Suite."

RED: Can you tell me what your favorite film signings at DD have been? You must have gotten all the major film names in there over the decades…

DH: We've had Roger Corman, Clive Barker, Ernest Borgnine, James Wan, all the Jasons, and most of the Michael Meyers at one point or another. The artists, composers, writers, cameramen, and anyone we can think of. They are all so very, very valuable in making this crazy horror world spin around.

RED: Is there anything left you want to do, that you haven't done yet?

DH: Although I've had Joe Hill and Christopher Rice, I have never had Anne Rice or Stephen King. Horror would never have been the same without them. We owe a debt to all of those people. I could sit here and recite names to you all the damn day long, and I'd still leave somebody out. As far as things I'd like to do beside more of what I already do? I'd like to act more. I'd love to be in a western. I'd like to direct a film. I said that to David Decoteau once and he said, "Yep, like we don't have enough directors." I think I did a spit-take. I love what I do, and I love that I'm able to share it and do it with my wife. You know, the signing events and the vast majority of stock in the store is all her, it's her sensibility. She just hates being in front of the camera, so somebody had to be the pretty face of Dark Delicacies. TA-DAH!

DAVID HEAVENER   ARIEL TEAL TOOMBS   AND RODDY PIPER

A FILM BY DAVID HEAVENER

LEGION: THE FINAL EXORCISM

TRUE FAITH VS. PURE EVIL

THE RETURN OF THE UNWATCHABLES

They Play in Theaters Now...

Greg Goodsell

Saturday, October 12, 2013: The Silent Movie Theater in Hollywood is packed to the rafters with hipster film fanatics this starry night. There is to be a screening of a double feature from a largely unsung "auteur" who has recently emerged from private life to meet with his many fans. Most of the people crowding the theater this night had yet to be born when these features were made, but became part of his appreciative fan base through word-of-mouth underground bootlegs and the rare VHS original, which fetches as much as $800 plus on the internet.

The fact that the auteur in question is not some rarefied European artiste, but independent contractor Chester N. Turner—and the films in question are his very entertaining, if roughshod shot-on-VHS Black Devil Doll from Hell (1984) and Tales from the Quadead Zone (1987)—is very remarkable. When this author wrote his original "Unwatchables" article for The Deep Red Horror Handbook nearly 30 years ago (on how many unschooled hands were picking up cameras to grind out product for video stores in the 1980s), Turner's Black Devil Doll from Hell was one of the chief exhibits on how outlandish, wrong-thinking features were then being given to an unsuspecting audience.

For those unfamiliar with the film, Black Devil Doll (shot-on-camcorder in the wilds of suburban Chicago) tells the tale of a young African American woman (played by Turner's then-girlfriend Shirley L. Jones) who is suddenly presented with life's possibilities after a plastic ventriloquist dummy with cornrows suddenly comes to life, ties her up, and rapes her. Yes, Black Devil Doll confronts the viewer with bad, haphazard home movie techniques to deliver an awful message (i.e. women secretly yearn for subjugation) that leaves the stricken audience member to ponder, "Why am I watching this?"

In between signing autographs that evening, Turner told this writer that yes, a female relative of his found his film "to be degrading to women." Turner qualified the film by saying that the likelihood of a plastic doll coming to life to give a wallflower her "heartfelt wish" was slim to none. True, true. One remembers how the United Kingdom banned Evil Dead (1982) over concerns that it would inspire corpses to reanimate and fly across rooms.

Black Devil Doll does address issues usually not seen in horror films, such as the hypocrisy of the African American church, the loneliness and isolation of single women, and the dominant/submissive dynamic found in most intimate relationships… and true to form, Black Devil Doll took all these issues and tore them up into a million pieces.

The memories of that night brought to mind yet another starry night several years earlier. Tuesday, April 25, 2006, to be precise, when Quentin Tarrantino's New Beverly Cinema screened Lawrence D. Foldes' Don't Go Near the Park (1979), a film I singled out for virulent anti-praise with its own special sidebar in my "Unwatchables" article. Park—about demonic modern-day cavemen who must mate incestuously with their offspring in order to be rewarded with eternal life—was a unique, all-over-the-map experience that fell beyond the means of the-then 19-year-old director, the results being a special sort of bad magic. The screening was sold out to an eager audience who saw the film's many flaws as something to be celebrated in an industry too often ruled by committee. The inebriated crowd laughed at all the right places, and Foldes, knowing of my special fascination with the film, tapped me on the shoulder in the thick of things to ask, "Is this your dream, Greg, finally seeing it on the big screen?" Indeed, it was.

While Park was originally something that Foldes wanted to consign to the past, with his Douglas Sirkian melodrama Finding Home (2006) on the cusp of being released, he was amazed (after an online search) at how many academic studies on the film saw through its gag-store gore to see the underlying themes of incest, abuse, and dysfunctional homes running throughout. The fact that the film was obviously directed by a 19-year-old didn't stop dark, mature themes from bubbling forward, and audiences responded.

The exciting thing today about no-budget films with big dreams far beyond the reach of their makers is that they are now attracting a theatrical, paying audience out for laughs and appreciative of singular, if highly skewed, visions. Bless Tommy Wiseau, the sweet-natured entrepreneur who disregarded advice to produce, direct, and star in The Room (2006). While laughing at bad movies has been around since the invention of the motion picture camera, Wiseau's The Room introduced the concept to millennials—and the torch has been passed on to a new generation.

This article will hopefully introduce the reader to some new Movie Gods and their Monstrous Projects. As before, one film in particular, Mark Region's After Last Season (2009) warrants its own section for stunning the viewer with its overreaching ineptitude. While others may say that this project "rewards bad behavior" by highlighting the work of bad filmmakers when the work of good filmmakers is going unnoticed, we're not going to let this get in the way of us having a good time, are we?

To begin—

VENTING BREEN

Exhibit Number One: Neil Breen, the living nightmare of what one would consider a fiercely independent filmmaker. Breen—somewhat resembling comedian Garry Shandling—writes, produces, and directs his features, starring himself... usually in the role of a Messianic Savior of Humanity.

Let that sink in.

Also take into consideration that Breen's day job comes from Las Vegas Real Estate. Now, let those four little words sink in, along with all the implications they carry.

Nothing will prepare the viewer for Breen's most famous feature, Fateful Findings (2009). A shot-on-video amalgamation of conspiracy theory, mundane suburban settings, and a one-two punch of delusions of grandeur coupled with a sky-high persecution complex, this is a movie that should be a lot more fun than it actually is. This writer hasn't seen Breen's other films, such as I Am Here... Now (2009), and frankly, I'm not in a rush. Judging by Fateful Findings, his other films must be as entertaining

as being trapped in an elevator with a doddering old man who badgers you with the parallels between current events, the Bilderbergers, and the War of 1812.

Fateful Findings begins with a stately tracking shot down a metallic corridor before landing on an ancient book on a pedestal. So far, so good... until gold sprinkles purchased from a nearby handcraft store begin to rain down on said book. Huh?

We then cut to a childhood memory of the story's protagonist, Dylan (Breen) frolicking in the forest with his childhood friend, Leah. In a quasi-mystical scene, a magical mushroom appears, accompanied by a small jewelry box filled with gumball machine trinkets. Sort of like Alejandro Jodorowsky, but not really. Leah exclaims, "It's a magical day!" and notes it in her handy notebook.

Dylan, now grown into adulthood as an angry young journalist, is struck by a car. Lots of close-ups of people's feet dominate this scene. Breen probably had trouble drafting extras that day. His wife (via cellphone) repeatedly says, "Dylan... talk to me! Dylan... talk to me!" Treated and released at a local hospital, he is unaware that his attendant nurse is his childhood friend, Leah—but she fits into the story later.

Back at his distressingly mundane suburban home, Breen rants that his next book will tear down idols in high places. His home office is especially telling, scattered with several fried laptop computers. Time passes... his best friend is shot and killed by his jealous wife, and she gets away with it. Dylan starts to see a psychiatrist. Dylan rebuffs the advances of an under-aged female suitor. He bickers with his wife over money.

Dylan begins seeing a second psychiatrist. Characters drink wine and pop prescription drugs. His second psychiatrist may be a ghost. By this time, the exasperated viewer will throw up their hands to ask, "Now, what does this have to do with the box of trinkets he found in the forest as a little boy?"

IT DOESN'T.

Eventually, Dylan meets Leah at a barbecue. She just so happens to have the very same notebook—remarkably well preserved— and they begin bonding again.

Long story short: nothing happens, and the nothing THAT DOES happen is particularly interesting. Dylan publishes his book, and world leaders around the globe graphically commit suicide to stirring, upbeat music. This montage is badly (and cheaply) done, but the whole sentiment behind it— that change through violent revolution can be a wonderful thing—is rather off-putting. (Can you think of anything positive that arose out of the Arab Spring?)

Breen "four-walls" his features—i.e., buys screen time at Southern California movie multiplexes (which we will find in common with a lot of filmmakers in this article)—to what is presumed to be a rather underwhelming response. This writer tried to track down Breen for an interview, to which he insisted take place at a nearby screening, and I thought the better of it.

Altogether, I can't really recommend Fateful Findings, as it exposes a stark truth that undermines this article at hand: bad films, by their very nature, are not entertaining.

"EAT THIS DOG SOUP!"

If Breen represents the type of independent filmmaker that one dreads is out there and active—a glorified egomaniac who casts himself as a Messianic savior in self-serving vanity projects—then Tom Charley represents the other side of the spectrum: home movies that are little more than angry, critical rants against everything that got in his craw the week of filming.

Charley has a few of these shot-on-video projects under his belt, his most famous being Song of the Blind Girl (2011), rightfully chosen by Hollywood's Silent Movie Theater as the most Holy Fucking Shit (HFS) project of the year.

To wit: a former Marine suffering from Post-Traumatic Stress Syndrome (Andrew Dawe-Collins) is stomping through the wilds of suburban Michigan when he commandeers a vacant home and begins restructuring his lost family with a series of kidnappings. His first victim, teenaged nymphet Jennifer (Madison Lehr), is snatched off the street. Holding her hostage, the vet shows that he means business by shooting a defenseless Bichon Friese and cooks it in a stew. "Eat this dog soup!" he bellows. His captive complies. "The dog was jumping in my stomach," she complains. "Now clean up that vomit! Here's a towel!" he barks.

Building his brood, our disgraced war hero snatches five-year-old Mia (Isabella Gielniak) from a shopping mall parking lot in broad daylight and tosses her into his trunk as indifferent shoppers breeze by. Mia and Mandy try to adjust to their perverse home arrangement as the outside world with its uncaring authority figures turn the other way to their plight. Director Charley has a lot on his mind and is unafraid of trouncing the audience's collective head with it. Inept policemen, nepotistic politicians, indifferent parents, and the State of Israel are to blame, Charley says, in scene after scene that recall the worst excesses of public-access television.

A rain of zany subplots ensues. The mother of Mia—"I thought I lost her in the parking lot!"— confesses to her daughter's murder, and then rescinds in order to protect her boyfriend, who she believes killed her. In the scene where the police grill the boyfriend (Mr. Miller), Song of the Blind Girl plays its most daring card. Miller, a Holocaust survivor denounces the detective as anti-Semitic and declares that the charges against him denigrates "the memory of 20 million genocide victims!" WHOA!

Under pressure to act on the kidnapped girls, authorities get a patsy to confess to the murders, whereupon police kill him in a hail of bullets. As a TV announcer puts it, "The suspect in the murder of Mia shot himself 72 times!"

Living in repressive conditions, the two girls begin to refer to their captor as "Daddy." After suffering morning sickness, Mandy confirms the worst with a home pregnancy test. "These things are like the weather forecast—always wrong! It's always the money! I'm glad I didn't pay for this!" the slimy vet says.

"Maybe I am pregnant, Daddy," Mandy says.

"How can you be pregnant? You're not even married!" he snarls.

"Well... there was this girl in my class and she was pregnant and she wasn't married," Mandy offers.

"That's from children from broken families and stuff. We don't have a broken family! Besides, you're too young to be pregnant!" he rationalizes.

And then, in a bit of unnecessary detail that would make the immortal Andy Milligan livid with envy, the veteran adds, "My cousin Cassandra, she had a stomach tumor... everybody thought she was pregnant, and then she died!"

This exchange is just one of countless others. You're going to have to see this to believe it, friends. Mandy becomes pregnant, and her captor talks her into self-inducing a coat-hanger abortion. Nearly dying from loss of blood, the girl's ordeal turns grimmer by the moment as the home's utilities are shut off and they contract pneumonia. Things get worse and worse and worse.

We'll cut to the chase: the veteran storms Mr. Miller's home, incensed by his clandestine underage prostitution ring, and points his rifle at him. "You can't do this to me! I'm a Holocaust survivor!" Miller pleads. Everybody dies horribly and the media disseminates lies, as in real life.

But seriously, folks—underneath its flamboyant nuttiness, Song of the Blind Girl appears to be addressing the needs of another, secret audience. Both girl actresses, attired in flimsy Daisy Dukes (and photographed in highly compromising poses at times) render Song of the Blind Girl, a film about child abuse in all true definitions of the term.

Song of the Blind Girl portrays an absolutely horrible world absolutely horribly— and I hear a stampede of feet rushing out to see it this very moment on the basis of that recommendation. Don't mess with director Charley's other movies, such as The President Goes to Heaven (2011). As rock singer Iggy Pop would croon, "No fun, my babe. No fun."

STOCKHOLM SYNDROME

Stockholm syndrome crops up in another hard-to-believe feature from 2011, The Abduction of Zack Butterfield. Shot on film, Butterfield is an ultra-low-budget number a bit more grounded in reality that still features plenty of moments to give the viewer... pause. Like Song of the Blind Girl, it addresses similar themes such as abduction, captivity, the sexual abuse of minors, and post-traumatic stress syndrome. But, as I shall soon reveal, you may not want to go rushing out to see this one, even if for educational purposes alone.

Blonde hottie April McKenna (Brett Halsham), returning from frontline combat in Iraq (and retiring to her bucolic country home in upstate New York), sets her sights on 14-year-old Zack Butterfield (TJ Plunkett). Why? Perhaps she sees Zack—a wet-behind-the-ears high school student—as a preferable alternative to the hardened military men around her. April neatly swipes him off the street during his morning jog. Kitting him out in a Battle Royale (1999) neck brace that threatens to explode on impact should he leave her home's perimeter, a sadistic tale of forced romance begins.

While cobbling bits of both Battle Royale and a lot from Misery (1990), another infamous tale of misplaced female affection, not an awful lot happens in Butterfield. Zack adapts to the situation rather readily. Three squares a day and light housework seems to be all that is required by his captor. Not much happens, and few things make sense. When the town's fat, elderly sheriff grills Zack's parents, the strangely composed mother and father misplace their priorities.

When the sheriff asks his parents about Zack's computer use, they note that he doesn't have a computer, because—in Zack's words—"He didn't type good."

"I would correct him and say, 'You don't type well,'" Zack's mother says. The dialogue then ruminates on the necessity of good grammar for a spell—at a time when they should be more concerned about their son being alive or dead. This choice bit of disjointed nonsense ranks right up there with After Last Season's "I've never been to that town, but I've been through it." [See sidebar.]

Lots of ho-hum non-action ensues, with Zack and April chit-chatting. When the inevitable happens (when the duo finally has sex) the camera points to the corner of the bed going up-and-down, up-and-down. After some more interminable scenes, Zack finally turns the tables and escapes, awaiting the police in a skimpy, store-bought Native American costume.

The Abduction of Zack Butterfield calls to mind the racy paperbacks that older brothers and fathers would slip to younger boys in order to initiate them into the mysteries of sex. Back in the '60s and '70s, drugstore shelves were full of quick-and-dirty paperbacks involving younger boys being seduced by older women. Freed from the more politically correct tenor of today—rape is rape, after all—these tawdry tomes would discretely dispense technical information intended for young men entering the sexual arena.

Now the bit of news I suggested at the beginning: go to Amazon.com, and type in The Abduction of Zack Butterfield. The DVD will pop up, and you will get all sorts of recommendations for like-minded movies. Look them over, and a queasy feeling that the film itself failed to deliver will bubble up. You will wonder if this isn't some sort of entrapment… if your name will be added to a list of People of Interest. You will back away suddenly, and hope that

no one took note… but then these movies will keep popping up, over and over again in your list of recommended titles. You've been warned.

HEAVENER TO BETSEY!

Anyone who has impulse-bought a DVD for $2.99 at a supermarket is intimately aware of the cinematic output of David Heavener. A highly prolific filmmaker operating far from the Hills of Hollywood, Heavener's titles span all genres, usually star him, and uniformly reek. His work in the horror and science-fiction genre includes Costa Chica: Confession of an Exorcist (2006), Evil Grave: Curse of the Maya (2004), Angel Blade (2002), and Outlaw Prophet (2001).

Perhaps the best introduction to Heavener is Outlaw Prophet. Heavener plays Jon 141, a headband-wearing Man from the Future, who darts about in futuristic laser-tag corridors at the local mall. The story weaves in Bible prophecy, numerology, and scenes of Heavener walking around a park talking to his kids.

As stated previously, Heavener operates far from the Hollywood Hills in the Tehachapi mountain range, near my hometown of Bakersfield, California. Intrigued by this fiercely independent filmmaker, I sought out Heavener for an interview in 2006. Meeting him at his home/movie studio/compound, Heavener entertained me with his showbiz stories and his plans to take on the lucrative internet streaming market. While a most gracious host, there were things about his production setup that made me… nervous.

With a few student films under my belt, I auditioned for Evil Grave: Curse of the Maya as a lark. Heavener was less than impressed with my reading, and cut me off in mid-sentence. He told me that he would stay in touch.

I won't go into great detail, but several of my other independent filmmaker friends sternly warned me against "wasting my time with him." I lost contact with Heavener after I declined an offer to travel 50 miles for a non-speaking role as an extra on my own time and dime.

Heavener keeps cranking 'em out, so somebody has to be watching his movies. They remain highly visible on the internet, where presumably they are watched by shut-ins with absolutely NOTHING to do. While serving up dicey chills and thrills, action, nudity, violence, and gore, half-baked theological discussions somehow work their way into all of Heavener's features. Check out this exchange between Heavener, playing an insufferably smug priest in Legion: The Final Exorcism.

HILLBILLY: Pastor John says that Catholic people don't know God and they can't have that personal relationship with God.

HEAVENER: Well, if that personal relationship with God means really knowing God, then how could one person know that person has a personal relationship with God? If, after all, it is personal.

HILLBILLY: Because Pastor John says so!

Heavener and the hillbilly have a brief tussle, some people arrive to break it up, and Heavener asks to use the can. And so on and so on.

For the curious, many of Heavener's movies can be seen for free on Amazon Prime. If you enjoy scintillating conversations like the one referenced above, zoom shots of pig faces to suggest a demonic presence, a Catholic church with stained-glass windows represented with chalk drawings on butcher paper, and Heavener's thespian skills, dig in! I'm going to pick up my dry cleaning.

IN SUMMATION...

With the digital revolution, many fans and quick buck artists are picking up their equipment to shoot their own features.

The good news is that some of these people are rising to the occasion to shoot the movies that they want to make, unfettered by the dictates of money-men and computer-generated imagery. The bad news is that the results are less than worthwhile, with amateur untrained hands trying to mimic current Hollywood successes. Does the world really need another found-footage fright flick?

Overall, amidst the dross, arrive some movies that positively stun the audience with their singular visions and odd choices—the results being much more entertaining than the latest installment of The Fast and the Furious.

And like all cultural anthropologists, we "outsider" film freaks are on the constant lookout for a new kick. The even better news is that these types of movies are playing in theaters now!

And that HAS to be a good thing!

"THERE'S UM, SOME PRINTERS IN THE BASEMENT THAT YOU CAN USE."

Making sense, um, of Mark Region's After Last Season

"The end of a season means... the beginning of a new one."

Websites are dedicated, interviews are conducted, reviews are offered, speculation arises... but nothing can prepare the audience for After Last Season (2009). Rendering the most enthusiastic fans of Tommy Wiseau's The Room (who faithfully toss plastic forks at the screen every weekend) into whimpering blobs of protoplasm, After Last Season threatens to engulf the audience in unmitigated, blah nothingness. Like Wiseau's vanity project, After Last Season is akin to the new type of film lighting up repertory movie theaters: misguided, personal projects from renegade filmmakers who don't get that the joke is on them. But make no mistake: After Last Season is quite unlike The Room or any other film ever, or never, made.

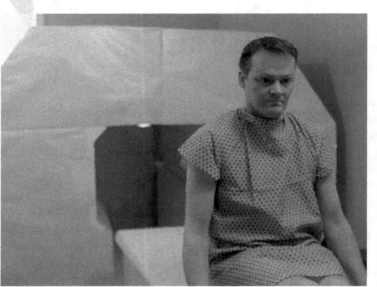

How to describe the alternate universe in which After Last Season is set? Characters are framed in the camera dead-center, overwhelmed by surrounding blank space, and lit harshly full-on with a single floodlight on non-color corrected 35mm film. "It's been many years since I've been in the area," one performer says. Plastic boxes are pulled across a rug with fishing wire. A ruler hangs in the air, held aloft by dental floss. "Oh, I've never been to that town, but I've been through it," another character says. One female actor has her hair brushed in front of her face in an attempt to disguise her participation. "There's, um, some printers in the basement you can use," says Matthew (Jason Kulas), the male lead. There is little to no musical score—the soundtrack is punctuated by the faraway sound of gurgling, akin to a toilet flushing two doors down. Mostly, there is lots and lots of crude computer animation, as if composed on an Amiga computer circa 1986. Lots and lots and lots of it.

Four-walled and playing in only four move theaters in the United States (Lancaster, California; North Aurora, Illinois; Rochester, New York, and Austin, Texas) for a single week, exhibitors were allegedly told to burn the prints afterward in lieu of sending them back to save on production costs. Breaking every single rule of conventional filmmaking, some assumed the film was just part of a viral campaign for Spike Jonze's Where the Wild Things Are (2009).

After Last Season struts into the audience's face to rudely slap away all previous expectations with the very first scene. An MRI machine is represented by a cardboard box cut with scissors and dressed with butcher paper and highly visible masking tape. The set itself—representing some sort of clinic—is a spare bedroom (painted "Little Princess Pink") with a ceiling fan. The fan is even awarded its own close-up. The final bits of art direction are 8 x 10 pieces of paper taped to the top of the wall in order to obscure the wallpaper borders. They threaten to fly away with a gust of wind from the fan.

Contrary to what has been written about the film, After Last Season does have a story, albeit one told so ineptly that it's easily obscured. There is a plague of murders affecting a small college town. The Prorolis Corporation (an indifferently framed building with the words burned into the film) is conducting mind experiments. Season's two main characters, Matthew and Sarah (Peggy McClellan) commence to experimenting, and stumble across the brainwaves of the killer. The majority of After Last

Season's running time consists of Matthew and Sarah's experiments that are represented by the aforementioned computer animation. If there are any real deal breakers with theatrical audiences with the film, they are these scenes. A revival of the film at Hollywood's Silent Movie Theater saw those galloping from the auditorium during these sequences being greeted by catcalls of "Chicken!" by braver souls.

Of all the internet reviewers describing Season's allure, perhaps the most eloquent was that the film is, "An accurate representation of how an autistic person sees the world."

Like most bad films that need to be seen several times, After Last Season's questionable artistic choices are steeped in mystery. Back to the MRI machine at the beginning. As one YouTube film reviewer would stridently declare, "Why didn't they just fucking go to a hospital and film a REAL MRI machine instead of settling for a cardboard box?"

"We made the sets simple," director Mark Region told Scott Macaulay in an online interview for Filmmaker Magazine. "I used shots of walls to show the passage of time in some scenes and to show that something is happening at a different location in other scenes. For the rest, we tried to keep the sets simple because of the budget."

Region added that the "way it happened, first we made the MRI, and it looked pretty good from far away. We couldn't tell it was made from cardboard or bits of plastic—it also has plastic. But when you shoot with 35mm, and sometimes because of the light, some lines across the front of the MRI became visible. When we shot, we couldn't tell, but on film the lines are darker—you see it's not a polished surface. That's how the MRI came to be."

Other memorable settings throughout the film include desks and tables made out of the aforementioned cardboard and brown wrapping paper, untreated drywall, and a ream of butcher paper tied around a pillar. Scenes filmed in actual houses, such as the ones seen in the beginning and end of the film, are sparsely decorated with bits gleaned from dollar store rummage bins.

But wait for it. According to various in-

FATEFUL FINDINGS
A NEIL BREEN FILM

ternet sources, After Last Season was produced for—gasp, choke—FIVE MILLION DOLLARS, incurred largely by the investors who insisted on four-walling the movie to theaters.

Other souls who have stumbled through After Last Season have asked this writer, "What were they thinking? How could such a monumentally inept and minimalistic movie get made and shown in theaters, on top of everything else?"

Having been around various independent film sets, I have a theory, maybe not true, but it's still a viable and intriguing theory. The people behind the film—and not necessarily just director Mark Region—saw the opportunity to make a feature film that was akin to TV's The X Files. The bits of pseudo-science tied into the avenging ghost subplot, along with the platonic investigative couple, would appear to bear this out.

Along the way, however, the filmmakers quickly realized that making a movie is a lot of hard work, and the inspiration that fueled the perspiration quickly evaporated. This would explain as to why the film was rushed out without color correction. It also appears (since everything is seen in long master shots) that the filmmakers had been meaning to go back and put in some close-ups later on, but didn't. The phrase, "We'll fix it in post," is thrown around a lot on indie movie sets. Tragically, rarely is it ever fixed in post.

I suspect that at one point, the people who were making the film threw up their hands and said, "This is going no place! I have the next level of this video game to get past first, anyway."

The film's investors, probably relatives and close friends of the filmmakers, then yelled in unison, "Oh, no you don't! We're too far into this financially now, and you're going to finish this picture or no more trust fund!"

The filmmakers resentfully comply, putting the least amount of effort into it as possible, cramming it with lots of extraneous, artless computer animation. The film is plopped into the hands of the distributors, it's seen by a disbelieving public, and some people hope that no one notices. Online interviews with the actors confirm that they were all paid scale for appearing in the film, which is currently $750 a day, minus taxes and agent fees, but have kept After Last Season off of their resumes.

[As a side note, director Region completed a short film, Medium Waves, immediately prior to Season. For some programmers, this feature has become a Holy Grail.]

The mystery that is After Last Season continues to baffle and intrigue. According to an online interview with one of the film's actors, "I still have friends who have managed to see it, and always ask me a million questions after viewing it... and I don't necessarily have all the answers for them. The whole journey has been an interesting process to reflect back upon."

Much like the creative talent behind the film, this writer has run out of cogent things to say. See it if you must.

TOBE WILL ALWAYS BE

Dennis Daniel

The summer of 2017 was rough on our beloved horror director icons. First, we lost George Romero, and then Tobe Hooper went off into that great goodnight.

The thing that feels so weird about it is that they've always kinda been here, ya know? Always around. Maybe not constantly active, but here nonetheless. There was always the chance they had one more masterpiece in them. Not that they owed anybody anything! They made their mark on the planet! Their work will live for as long as people give a shit about great works of art in the horror genre.

It still kills me that there are people walking around who don't know who the Marx Brothers are. And while millennials may not know these guys by name, I'm almost positive that they know, have heard of, or have seen Night of the Living Dead and The Texas Chain Saw Massacre.

Many, many years ago, I wrote a column for Deep Red called "Tobe or Not Tobe". I had not been a huge fan of the Texas Chain Saw sequel (my opinion has changed drastically over the years; I love it now), but at the time, I was expecting something more horrific, gory, and less... uh... funny? Leatherface in love?

So, I went on and on about how Tobe had not fulfilled the promise of what the director of TTCSM might do next. I listed all

of his films up until that point, and pretty much dissed them. Yes, Poltergeist was pretty cool, but it was too Spielbergian to have his original stamp on it.

But this is not about what Tobe did or didn't do right, or what I personally may feel were his weak points as a director. FUCK WHAT I THINK! This is the guy who directed The Texas Chain Saw Massacre, and if that was the only thing he ever did in his life, we'd still be mourning his passing.

As many Deep Red brethren and sistren may remember, TTCSM was our late, great editor Chas Balun's favorite film. Think about that! Of all the films he wrote about

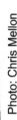

Photo: Chris Mellon

have a gigantic fat-ass maniac wearing other people's faces chasing after you with a chainsaw in the middle of the night!

Everything about TTCSM is memorable. EVERYTHING! It is non-stop fucked up from the get-go. Relentless in its uncomfortableness. Unceasing in its images. Mind-numbing in its surprises and plot twists. You are never safe. EVER. Even the opening narration, the sounds of those camera clicks, and the quick corpse reveals are unnerving... to this day! You could show that film to the most gore-obsessed geeks going, and they'd applaud it from beginning to end. For sheer horror chutzpah, it just can't be beat. So fucking groundbreaking for 1974!

I can't tell you how many versions of it I've owned—from VHS, to LaserDisc, to DVD, and now the Blu-ray. It is a gorgeous looking film in its colorful, grainy glory. It is so in your face. The documentary style is beyond off-putting. And, what a title! Perhaps my favorite title in all horrordom!

Like so many masterpieces, many have

and all the gore-meister delights he praised... his favorite was the one where there was hardly a drop of blood! We all know why! It was because of Tobe's genius.

The suggestion of horror and the quick cut that makes you think that you saw something that you didn't see is the very key to the film's impact. It also helps to

tried to duplicate The Texas Chain Saw Massacre. Even Tobe himself! The only one I've ever really liked is TTCSM: The Beginning (2006). But that hasn't stopped me from owning every one of them!

WHO WILL SURVIVE AND WHAT WILL BE LEFT OF THEM?

My hope for the future is that Tobe's name will survive... and that what will be left of him is one fucking astonishing accomplishment! May his name live forever in the annals of horror.

TOBE HOOPER. REST IN PIECES.
(I think that would have made him chuckle...)

TERROR TALES AND BLOODY THINGS!

An interview with Eerie Pubs historian Mike Howlett

John Szpunar

When Feral House announced the arrival of Mike Howlett's The Weird World of Eerie Publications in 2010, I almost fell out of my chair. I'd seen a few of the Eerie mags here and there, but I never paid them much attention. To me, the most memorable things about them were their titles (Tales from the Tomb, Weird, Tales of Voodoo, et al) and their cover art—a cornucopia of lurid paintings that left even the slightest notion of good taste dead in the dirt.

Still, I was always intrigued by the things. What had I been missing? I'd always assumed that the Eerie Pubs operated on such a subterranean level that even the worms avoided them. Weren't they just poor knock-offs of the far superior Warren and Skywald titles? Didn't their artists just swipe and retouch the artwork from lesser-known horror pre-codes? And who were the artists, anyway?

I knew a little bit about Myron Fass, the renegade publisher behind the mags. I knew that Carl Burgos, the creator of The Human Torch, served as the editor. I knew that James Warren, the publisher of Creepy, went toe-to-toe with Fass when he launched its sister (er… cousin) mag, Eerie. And… well, that's about all I knew. It was time to take a step off the beaten path and pay these things a visit.

The Weird World of Eerie Publications is one of the most fascinating documentations of horror comics history that has ever been published. Volumes have been written

HAVE YOU EVER HAD THE URGE TO DO SOMETHING DARING OR SHOCKING... SOMETHING THAT WOULD MAKE PEOPLE TAKE NOTICE OF YOU? THEN YOU CAN PROBABLY UNDERSTAND THE EMOTIONS THAT WERE INVOLVED WHEN FRANK ANNOUNCED...

I CHOPPED HER HEAD OFF!

about the ECs and their mutant children, but little has ever been said about the Eerie Pubs, due in large part to the fact that there was no solid information about them to be had. It seemed as if everyone was as in the dark about them as I was.

And then, Mike Howlett came a-knocking at that old dark house and kicked the door wide open.

Meet Myron Fass, the gun-toting eccentric whose uncanny ability to cash in on a trend created a publishing empire. Meet Carl Burgos, the grizzled industry vet who

went from Marvel to mayhem with a fierce and fiery grin. And meet the artists themselves, both seasoned pros and Argentinean up-and-comers who lived by the law of "More blood!" as they penciled and inked their way into the night.

I read the book in a marathon sitting, smiling wickedly as all of my questions about the Eerie Pubs were answered. A gargantuan gap in horror comics history had suddenly been filled. I set the book down, picked up a pen, and started scribbling down questions. It was now time to talk to the author himself to find out just how in the hell he did it…

DEEP RED: When did you become interested in horror comics?

MIKE HOWLETT: We always had comics in the house as a kid. The horror ones were the ones that I liked. I can remember House of Mystery and Tales of the Unexpected, the old 12 and 15-centers. I used to make those old Creepy Crawlers.

RED: Creepy Crawlers?

MH: You know, the toys where you'd make those bugs. In the mid '60s, I'd make the bugs and sell them to kids on the way home from school so I could go out and buy comic books. I've been a horror geek forever.

RED: [Laughs] Were you able to capitalize on your endeavor?

MH: Yeah, I'd sell them for a couple cents

Before and after...

apiece. Once I had 20 cents, I'd close shop and run down to get the latest House of Secrets, or whatever was there. It kept me going.

RED: When were you first exposed to the pre-codes?

MH: Well… do you remember The Monster Times?

RED: Of course. Joe Kane was the editor for most of its run.

MH: Yeah. I picked up issue #10 because I was obsessed with the Tales from the Crypt movie, just from seeing an ad on TV. And issue #10 was all about EC horror comics. As soon I saw that, I was like, "Oh, man!" So that was my first exposure to what had come before.

RED: The ECs certainly set a benchmark, but I'm curious about what you thought of the other titles—stuff from Harvey and Ajax, and things like that.

MH: Well, I started buying ECs back when I moved to Boston in 1980. There was a store that had a few of them. Then, I started going to some conventions and learning

> *"I would recognize a story from Black Cat Mystery or something from Harvey. The Harvey comics were pilfered for hundreds of stories."*

about some of the other titles that were out there. Over the years, I've collected most everything that I wanted. But yeah, I love Harvey and Ajax, and I certainly couldn't have done the Eerie Publications book without having some rough knowledge of the Ajax titles. I love all of the off-brand stuff. You can only read the ECs so many times—I can quote half of the stories. But the stories for Mysterious Adventures and Dark Mysteries—when those guys were on, they were as good as the ECs. I like the really base and gruesome stuff. I don't even care about the artwork sometimes, as long as it's pushing buttons and ballsy.

RED: The Eerie Pubs certainly fit that bill. To tell you the truth, I knew next to

nothing about them before I read your book.

MH: That's why I wrote the book. I didn't know anything about them either. I was like, "These things are really weird." There was no information on them. As soon as I found out that Dick Ayers had done some of the stories, I started going to some shows in New York that he was at. I started writing to him, asking, "Who are these people?" He was such a great springboard.

RED: For those who might not know who Dick Ayres is, could you say a little something about him?

MH: Well, he was a comic book legend, I guess. He was probably best known for inking Jack Kirby. Pretty much anybody who has picked up a comic book has enjoyed his artwork. I guess Ayres was one of Kirby's favorite inkers, and they did all of those giant monster comics back in the late '50s. What can you say about Ayres? He's was around since the '40s and there are reams and reams of pages with his artwork on it.

RED: I take it you were a fan of the War-

ren and Skywald magazines…

MH: I collected all the black and white stuff. And I loved the Skywalds. I've got to say, they're probably my favorite of the bunch. I had some Eerie Pubs lying around, but they were printed very cheaply. They're pretty garish and, frankly, a little ugly. They really didn't float my boat as much. But they were down and dirty. How did they dare put this stuff out to compete? And then I realized that Dick Ayres was one of the artists. I was like, "Wow. He was slumming it!" But, thank god he was. Some of his stuff is so bloodthirsty and over the top. I later found out that Chic Stone, another Marvel artist, was slumming. It's kind of fascinating that they would lower their standards. But were they really lowering their standards or just exploring a different avenue?

RED: Chic Stone was still working for Marvel, right?

MH: Oh yeah. So was Dick Ayres. Both of them were still concurrently at Marvel. That's why they weren't signing their work.

RED: You mentioned that your favorite publisher from that era was Skywald. What was it about them that put them ahead of the game?

MH: I liked Al Hewetson, the editor. I liked his style of writing, and he did write most of the stuff. It was very descriptive and oozing with purple prose. He was very H.P. Lovecraft with his descriptions. It was pure horror. It wasn't modern, but it [somehow] was. There was this dark past coming up to haunt you. It was very florid, but I kind of dug it because it let the artists go crazy. There was a bit of a mean-spiritedness, but it was all in good fun. And also, it pissed my father off when he looked at an issue. I think it was a story called "Make Mephisto's Child Burn" where they're burning a witch at the stake. She's pregnant and she gives birth, pushing the baby out away from the flames—and they throw it back in! He came down and said, "This is SICK!" The Skywalds were also kind of fun because they would have the readers write in about nightmares and they'd illustrate them. They were very reader friendly, which was attractive to me.

RED: I thought Skywald was great because they introduced me to a lot of artists that I hadn't heard of before.

MH: Yeah. Like Maelo Cintron, the "Hu-

man Gargoyles" guy. To this day still, who has heard of him? It was beautiful, beautiful stuff.

RED: So, what attracted you to the Eerie Pubs?

MH: I wanted to learn more about them. I don't know how I'd gone so long, but sometime around the mid '80s, I saw that cover of Weird that Chic Stone did with that guy with two heads. He's cutting off a girl's head. In the background, there's a bunch of ghoul-hippies with signs: "DOWN WITH VIOLENCE!" "LOVE, NOT HATE!"

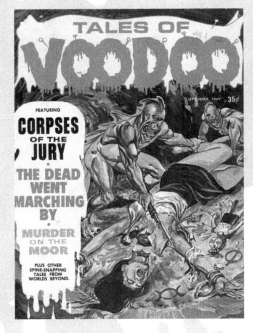

They're looking on at the gore scene, and are drooling with glee. It's such an over-the-top cover. I said, "OK, I've got to learn more about these things. In 1969, this thing was sitting on a newsstand. Why?"

RED: A foreshadowing or a reaction to Altamont? It's kind of mind-boggling.

MH: The juxtaposition is pretty great.

RED: You have to wonder what was going through the minds of the guys who were drawing those covers. Were you able to get any insight into that?

MH: Well, I couldn't talk to any of the cover artists. Chic Stone has passed away. I finally figured out who Bill Alexander was—he was their main cover artist. I was never able to find him or a family member. I haven't given up trying, though. I've got a book coming in his honor one of these days; he's got such a huge body of work. But ultimately, it was all due to Myron

Fass, the publisher. He wanted the gore.

RED: Sensationalism—you have to outsell the competition.

MH: Yeah. Severed heads and shoulders above the rest! [Laughs] Fass was a wild publisher. He took everything to the nth degree in whatever genre he was putting magazines out. And he did them all. He was putting out National Enquirer-type magazines and the covers of those things were insane. "I BLEW A PROSTITUTE TO BITS!" screamed the headlines. It was sensationalism, whatever would sell. The comics? Let's make them as gory as possible. The H.G. Lewis movies made a lot of money, so…

RED: Exactly. And the Eerie Pubs aren't that far removed from the H.G. Lewis films. How did Myron Fass get started in publishing?

MH: Myron was a pre-code horror artist who was, wisely, always looking to EC for inspiration. He did a lot of art swipes from the superior EC artists. He did a lot of great stories—a lot of mean-spirited, down and dirty horror stuff in the '50s. Once the code came in, there wasn't a lot of room for an artist with his particular set of strengths. He still did a little bit of it, but he decided to move over to publishing. Once again looking to EC, he put out a MAD knock-off called Lunatickle.

RED: I've never seen an issue. Was it any good?

MH: It was pretty much a knock-off of what MAD was at the time. Color cover, black and white inside, twenty-five cents. They didn't have the writing that MAD had, but some of the artists were pretty good. Fass himself drew some of it, and he could hold his own.

RED: How long did it last?

MH: It lasted for two issues, but it really did whet his appetite for the publishing game.

RED: I like to think about how wild and wooly the publishing game was back then. There was a set number of legitimate titles and everyone else was imitating them and trying to latch on, almost driving things into the ground.

MH: Yeah. And eventually, that's what did in the Eerie Pubs themselves. Fass was never a leader, but he was always a really

CURSE of the VAMPIRE

quick follower. If a trend is popular, the first people mocking that trend stand to make a lot of money. And he did. After Lunatickle folded, he jumped into girlie mags. Playboy was making a mint and he was doing some of the girlie digests.

RED: James Warren originally started off with a nudie magazine…

MH: Yeah. After Hours. Those were pretty good, too. But Fass was just jumping onto whatever trend was hot at the time. Later in the decade when Famous Monsters came out, he put out Shocking Tales, Suspense, and Monster Parade.

"And then I realized that Dick Ayres was one of the artists. I was like, Wow. He was slumming it! But, thank god he was."

RED: I don't think I've ever seen a copy of Monster Parade.

MH: It wasn't anything like Famous Monsters, but it had monsters in it. It was also a little bit unsavory—girls in their knickers getting eaten by werewolves and stuff like that.

RED: Fass eventually started stepping on Warren's turf.

MH: Creepy had come out and it was making a lot of money. Once again, Fass was one of the first ones to jump on the bandwagon. "I want to get in on this, too. I'll call mine Eerie." Warren had already advertised another magazine called Eerie, and there was a fight between Fass' backers and Warren. There's a good story in the book about that. Warren did get the name, in a legendary story about overnight publishing. How true it really is, nobody knows. I guess it's been exaggerated a lot over the years.

RED: That was something that really fascinated me as a kid. I loved to read the fine print in the Overstreet Comic Book Price Guide that explained things. I was like, "Oh man... I'm never going to find a copy of that thing!"

MH: Have you?

RED: No. I kind of quit looking.

MH: [Laughs] I printed my own copy of it years ago.

RED: I used to have dreams that I'd find it in a flea market somewhere.

MH: It's a fantasy that we all have and will continue to have until it actually happens. You still hear about it sometimes—the old lady with a box of funny books in her closet.

RED: When did you decide that you wanted to write a book about the Eerie Pubs?

MH: I have a friend in England named Peter Normanton who does a fanzine called From the Tomb. I'd written a couple of things for him over the years and enjoyed doing the research for them. I said, "Hey, I'm looking to do another article for you. What do you think is more important, something on the Red Circle horror comics (there were about six issues, with a couple of titles that had great Gray Morrow artwork) or Eerie Pubs?" He said, "I've had a lot of requests for something on the Eerie Publications." I started looking into it, and I realized that there was nothing written about them. You couldn't search the web and find very much. Tom Brinkman, who put out Bad Mags for Headpress, had about the only information on Myron Fass. But the more I dug, the more these spider webs of avenues to search opened up. I started to realize that this was so much more than a five-page article. I emailed Peter and said, "I hope I'm not leaving you in the lurch, but I think I might have a book here. This thing just keeps growing." This was only after a couple of months.

RED: You mentioned that Dick Ayres was a big help.

MH: Yeah. It was mostly due to him. He gave me these springboards. Some of the only information you could find online was misinformation. Ezra Jackson's name is in every Eerie Pub as art director. Somewhere, somebody started saying that he was really Myron Fass and that Ezra Jackson was a pseudonym. I was thinking, "Well, this is another avenue to pursue." Then, Dick

Ayres said, "Yeah, Ezra Jackson was a really good artist and he had it really tough." I asked, "Why is that?" Ayres said, "He was a black man trying to find jobs in a fairly white-knit community." I was like, "Oh. Well, that's not Myron Fass, then!" Every little bit of information opened up new avenues. It became an obsession of four, five, six years of writing. Once I discovered that most of the new artists were from Argentina, it put a whole new wrinkle on things. A lot of those guys were youngsters just trying to get some work in an American magazine.

"He was a gun enthusiast, and some of the people that I interviewed wouldn't talk to me about him or his practices. Even though he was dead, they were still afraid of him."

RED: The fact that guys from Argentina were working for Myron Fass really boggled my mind.

MH: Well, it was good work and it was cheap. They could pay peanuts for seven pages of artwork from some studio in Argentina, and the studio and the artists were happy because the dollar was strong. They

were probably getting a pretty decent paycheck per page.

RED: A lot of the artwork in the Eerie Pubs was swiped from 1950s pre-codes. How difficult was it to pin down where the stories originally appeared?

MH: I had a method, and I've got to say that many years of work went into it. I would recognize a story from Black Cat Mystery or something from Harvey. The Harvey comics were pilfered for hundreds of stories. I'd grab that issue and write down the story title and a little synopsis—mostly just the beginning and the very last panel. I kept a little catalogue. Eventually, I went through every Harvey and every synopsis. I had them all; I've been collecting these things for years. By going through those synopses and by going through the Eerie Pubs over and over and over again, I matched something like over 600 stories.

RED: That's a lot of work!

MH: I matched all but about 10. I had a lot of help from other collectors: "Hey do you have this and I don't. Can I just get the splash and the final page scanned?"

RED: What kind of guidelines were the artists given to adapt these things?

MH: I can tell you what Dick Ayres told me—none of the Spanish people will really admit to it. Well, it's not that they don't admit to it; they did it a little differently, perhaps. But Dick Ayres said that Carl Burgos and Fass gave him tear sheets, which were essentially xeroxed copies of a pre-code horror story. They said, "Just keep all the words. We'll give it a new title. Draw the artwork and interpret it any way that you want." Sometimes the Ace titles like Web of Mystery were a little verbose, so Burgos would cross out a couple of lines that weren't necessary. "Keep the reading down! Who wants to do that? We just want to look at the pictures!" Some of the artists in Argentina probably didn't understand English all that well, so they kept really close to the layout and the format. People like Dick Ayres, Chic Stone, and Larry Woromay would kind of go off in crazy directions. One guy, Hector Castellon, who also did a couple of things for Warren, would take the plot and make a new story. But yeah, they were given xeroxed copies with orders to make it bloodier.

RED: I guess Fass and Burgos must have given the artists orders to rip open

faces and gouge out eyeballs…

MH: [Laughs] Dick Ayres said, "I must be the eye poppin' guy!" I'd like to think that Ayres kind of came up with the popping eyes and tongues and Jackson said, "Well, he's got that. I'm going to come up with the ripped open cheek, with the teeth exposed!"

RED: I got the impression that Myron Fass was the Phil Spector of the publishing world.

MH: Yeah, that's a good description. To say he was eccentric is putting it very mildly. He was a gun enthusiast, and some of the people that I interviewed wouldn't talk to me about him, or his practices. Even though he was dead, they were still afraid of him. Evidently, he would go from desk to desk at 9:00 on a Monday morning. He would tap his gun on the desks. "Hey, where's Steve? He's not in yet!" (TAP, TAP, TAP…) He would really intimidate people, not only with his boss power, but by packing heat. People would walk in on Monday morning and there'd be all of these red pellets all over the floor because he was taking target practice on Sunday in the office. He really fancied himself as a gunslinger. Even back in the '50s when he was drawing, he did some artwork for Lev Gleason's Black Diamond Western. He was a pretty good western artist and he did a couple of covers where there's a guy with a big nose and glasses who looked a little like Myron himself. He said that he was decorated by the New York police as a crack shot.

RED: Well, he sure sold himself as one.

MH: Absolutely. He could sell anything. He was selling his persona, as well. He did a lot of gun mags. This was in the late '70s, and he did the product reviews himself as a professional who knew his stuff.

RED: How hard was it come by some of the later things that he put out?

MH: It was really hard, especially after he left the northeast and went down south. There are a couple of years where he's hard to trace. But, I found a few people who worked with him down there going through the credits pages. Things hadn't actually changed too much; he was publishing out of the back of a gun shop. One guy said that he told him, "You should be happy to know that you're working on the number one selling monthly gun magazine… in Brazil!" So, he was at least selling enough

to put out the next issue. Tom Brinkman told me that he was going until the '90s, but I haven't been able to find anything after the mid '80s. I don't have the titles, but I don't doubt that he was getting something out. A guy told me that he was still doing girlie mags and having the models come in and change in the bathroom. Never a dull moment in the Fass regime!

RED: The book is beautiful. How did you get in touch with Feral House?

MH: Well, I had the book pretty much done. I had some more research to do, but I thought I was close enough to present it to somebody. They were my first choice.

"One day, I got an email from him. He said, "How about I re-draw one of the things that I did or draw an all new one?"

It's a Man's World and Sin-A-Rama are beautiful books. I love the printing, and I love the hard covers and the glossy pages. And with the Eerie Pubs, you can't just reproduce the covers in black and white. It's all about the gore—you've got to have that red. I've heard the covers described as sideshow banners, and you wouldn't want that in black and white. That really informed my decision and I sent a query to Adam Parfrey. He agreed with me that it might

be a good fit because it's certainly very exploitable. That's what it's all about, in the tradition of Fass himself.

RED: How was Adam to work with?

MH: It was awesome. He pretty much let me do what I wanted to do. First of all, he hooked me up with Sean Tedjarati, the designer. He's beyond genius—I lucked out so bad. We had a blast talking on the phone—he's in Los Angeles and I'm on the East Coast. We'd set up each chapter tentatively and Adam would look at it. Sometimes he'd say, "I want this picture to lead off the crime chapter—the guy with his eyeball getting blown out." Well, I can live with that! But he let me keep my words, as is. He even hooked me up with Joe Coleman, who's a friend of his. Joe had some Myron stories. This was after we'd already started the layout. It was great stuff; I couldn't not put it in.

RED: The covers to the Eerie Pubs have a Coleman style to them.

MH: Oh, yeah. I can see a definite influence. One of the very last things that Myron and his brother put out was the reprinted Gasm magazine, repackaged as Rump. There's one with a Joe Coleman cover that I'm very glad to have fit into the book.

RED: You also got Dick Ayres to draw an original story for the book.

MH: One day, I got an email from him. He said, "How about I re-draw one of the things that I did, or draw an all new one? It's your discretion, whatever you want to do." Basically, he was looking for a gig. [Laughs] I didn't really have the money to do it, but I told him I'd keep it in mind. And the more I thought about it, the more I thought, "He's right. For me to make this book everything it can be, I've got to have it in there." I already knew what I wanted him to do. I wanted him to draw Horror of Mixed Torsos.

RED: A classic! What was the experience like?

MH: It was fascinating for me to hear him talk about it. He would email me updates saying, "This is just like working for Carl and Myron! I've got the lettering done, and I'm working on the layout!" He was really excited, and that made me feel really good. He was 86 years old at the time, and he was all excited about an art gig.

RED: The fact that his hand was as steady as it was when he did it is amazing.

MH: Yeah. I had one person complain that it looked like he rushed it. No, he didn't. It took him a few weeks. And we struck up a great friendship. We had dinner a couple of times. It was awesome to pick the guy's brain.

RED: How did Steve Bissette become involved with the project?

MH: He was doing a comic show in New Hampshire, and I went up with a couple of books for him to sign. I told him about what I was working on. We got to talking about the Eerie Pubs and he drew me a picture of a zombie with its eyeball popping out. I said, "Are you interested in writing an intro?" He said, "Absolutely." He loves the stuff, and there are not too many of us out there that would admit to it. It doesn't say much for me, but a lot of people say that his intro is the best part of the book. It's really told from a fan's point of view, from seeing these things on the newsstand at the time.

RED: I thought it worked really well. You get a fan's perspective on things, and then you dive into the meat and potatoes of your research.

MH: It worked for me, too. The only thing that I could draw from my childhood was trading a copy of Horror Tales for a Rolling Stones 45. [Laughs]

RED: Now that I've read your book, I have an education on things. Like I said, I was really clueless about the Eerie Pubs before I started reading.

MH: That's awesome. That's why I did it. I didn't know much about it either, and once I started finding things out, I thought that everyone should know about this stuff. It's an interesting story and these unknown artists deserve some sort of credit.

RED: On that note, do you think you have every Eerie Pub catalogued and accounted for?

MH: I have never found anything else. There are a couple of other collectors who think they have full runs and our lists are the same. I've always said that I wouldn't be surprised if something else turned up but as far as I know, I've got it all.

RED: How long did it take you to compile your second book, The Weird Indexes of Eerie Publications?

MH: I had initially planned to have the in-dexes in the Weird World book, but there just wasn't enough room for them. A good chunk of the six years that I was working on that book was spent gathering info for the indexes. It was put together a little at a time, as information presented itself.

RED: How has it been selling?

MH: The indexes are really only for the hardcore fan. I have been thrilled that a

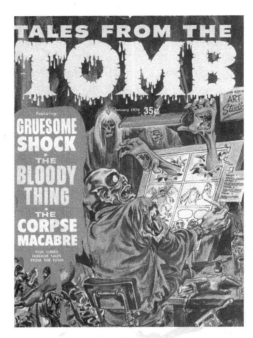

"All of these artists were real professionals, but the work looked like crap because it was printed so poorly."

couple of hundred copies have sold. It's a made-to-order book on Lulu.com, and I have it priced cheaply. Every once in a while, I get a check from Lulu for $17 or so, so I can't complain. I just wanted to get the info out there for people to use while shopping for Eerie Pubs.

RED: Putting something like that together would have driven me insane…

MH: It was all part of the research for the Weird World book, so I was already well beyond insanity. [Laughs] I actually kind of like the making of notebooks and compiling data, as long it's for fun stuff like comic books and not actual work!

RED: How did you meet Craig Yoe?

MH: I met Craig at the New York Comic Con during my pre-release huckstering phase for the Feral House book. He had just had his first Chilling Archives book come out, the Dick Briefer one. I bought it and gave him a T-shirt that I'd made to promote my forthcoming book. Not sure if it worked, but he did wind up buying my book when it came out, and he gave me a glowing review. We formed a bit of a mutual admiration society and have become fast friends in the past few years. He's one of the good people on the planet, and I would do anything for him.

RED: How did The Worst of Eerie Publications (IDW, 2014) come about?

MH: Craig wanted to work with me and pitched the idea. IDW gave us a green light, so we went ahead with it. He gave me complete freedom to do whatever I wanted. He also let me use my friend Jason Willis to put it together, so I was in very good design hands. Jason has an amazing vision… if you haven't seen his animated Eerie Pubs meets the Johnson-Smith Novelty Company "Horror Record" video, go watch it NOW! His award-winning Catnip: Egress to Oblivion film is genius. But I digress…

RED: How did you go about picking the tales that are included in the book?

MH: I wanted stories that were representative of their output. Of course, I wanted lots of gore. Chic Stone's "Blood Bath" and Dick Ayers' "I Chopped Her Head Off" were no brainers. I picked many of the "classics"—stories that we Eerie Pub nerds always talk about. I also wanted to have a mixture of the artists, with a good sampling of the Argentinian crew, as well as the Americans.

RED: Can you explain the restoration process of reprinting the stories? I've always been fascinated by that sort of thing.

MH: I scanned everything at 600 dpi. I then put it into good ol' Paint. I've never used Photoshop or Gimp or anything. Just Paint. I wouldn't know how to use Photoshop, but I kick ass on Paint.

Now, the Pubs were printed on shitty paper—so the first pass was to clean up all of the pock-marks. Then I would solidify the blacks, which would invariably be compromised because of the lousy ink they used.

I would do this on full size, maybe about 1/32 of the page on the screen at a time. It took about two years to clean it all up to my satisfaction. Craig was going nuts.

RED: [Laughs] I can imagine!

MH: The Pubs used a lot of grey wash to add shadows. I tried to choose first-prints of some stories, before they added the wash for the reprinting. On a story with the washes, the image would break up when I had it at the humongous size I was working on. I found myself having to reconstruct voice balloons and caption blocks—even text and dialog. But I felt it was worth it to present the artwork in the best possible light. These mags were slammed for years for having subpar artists, but it's really not the case. All of these artists were real professionals, but the work looked like crap because it was printed so poorly. I'm really happy with the result. And yes, I fixed the spelling on a few words. So sue me!

RED: What led up to Snake Tales (IDW, 2016)?

MH: Craig and I were both guests at FantaCon 2015, and our tables were together. (Keeping the riff-raff from the celebrities!) A friend of his, Dr. Frank Burbrink, came by and was shopping for horror comics, of which I had a box for sale. My true passion is wildlife, and snakes are a favorite animal of mine. Frank had just been appointed Curator in the Department of Herpetology at the American Museum of Natural History. He is basically living my dream, and we hit it off, talking snakes and horror comics.

RED: Was the project your idea?

MH: It was Craig's. He was listening to us talk, and a lightbulb went on over his head. I was eager to do the book, though, because I am an advocate for snake conservation, and I wanted to get a little education into the book as well. You see, the science in the pre-code books is all hogwash… snakes are always evil killing machines or some unsavory monster. I wanted to give some truth in my intro to counteract the bullshit in the stories. Fun bullshit, but still bullshit. I was very happy to see Frank going in the same direction in his forward [for the book].

RED: Again—how did you settle on which stories to include?

MH: We had a ton of potential stories. Steve Banes, who edits the essential Haunted Horror comic for Yoe Books, was helping

us find stories. His knowledge and memory are astounding. He got my favorite credit ever in Snake Tales… Boa Consultant. He really was very helpful with ideas and scans.

I wanted good art, exciting stories, and as much variation as possible. We probably could have done a whole book of Medusa stories, but I finally settled on just one, Hy Eisman's "Medusa". Craig also likes to

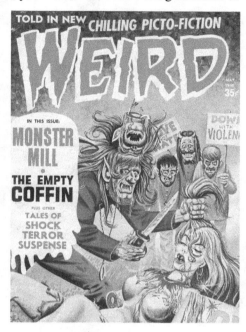

"As we speak, I'm finishing up the long-planned Eerie Pubs cover book. It will be every Eerie Pubs cover chronologically."

have some sex appeal in his books, so the snake-goddess theme is well represented. It broke my heart to cut some of the stories, but we had to keep the page count reasonable or nobody would be able to afford the book! I think we wound up with a good selection of exciting stories with some killer art.

RED: What is working with Craig Yoe like?

MH: I love Craig and Clizia. They let me do whatever I want. Of course, they have to pull me back down to earth sometimes, but we have an excellent working relationship.

We're good friends and we respect each other a lot. Our book talks are kind of like two kids in a tree fort making plans for an afternoon.

RED: I take it that you're going to continue to work with them…

MH: Yeah, I'm officially a slave in the Yoe dungeon. As we speak, I'm finishing up the long-planned Eerie Pubs cover book. It will be every Eerie Pubs cover chronologically. I've had many fans suggest this book to me over the years and I finally got off my butt and got it started. Look for it late 2017 or early 2018.

RED: A few years ago, you told me that you were thinking about writing a book on Crown International Pictures. Is it still in the works?

MH: The Crown project became pretty overwhelming. It had to take a back seat to some of my Yoe projects and other pursuits, but I'm still gathering information when I find it. The people who still keep Crown alive haven't wanted anything to do with me, despite queries and even bribing them with my Eerie Publications book. I tried to let them know that it would be a respectful tome. I adore their output.

So, the project is alive but just simmering on the back burner while I decide when I'll have enough time to give it the attention it deserves. Writing about film is surprisingly very different from writing about comics, and I have to become more comfortable doing it.

RED: What are your future plans?

MH: Other than the Crown idea, there's nothing etched in stone. Craig has asked me to do a couple more books and has given me carte blanche, which is both a blessing and a curse. "I can do whatever I want! But just what the hell do I want?"

RED: I know the feeling!

MH: We're looking at the possibility of another full series reprint like we've done with Ajax-Farrell's Voodoo. As interesting things come up, I'll try to keep my chops up writing for fanzines.

Mostly, I'll just continue to be a fan. That's how you learn the most; enjoy different things and immerse yourself in them. Be it nature, horror films, comics, music… whatever. Just enjoy it, let it in and let it become a part of you…

HAND IT TO REMO
WIN, LOSE OR DRAW

Shane M. Dallmann

It was the early 1970s and I was in the second grade. I wanted to draw my own comic books. My inspiration (of course) came in the form of the classic cartoons I watched on Saturday mornings, but my characters were the classic monsters that I watched on Saturday nights (when I was lucky). My first monster cartoon, therefore, involved Dracula getting the hiccups. The Count went through all the remedies that countless other cartoon characters had already tried (holding his breath, drinking a glass of water, etc.). But then he saw a huge crucifix hanging on his wall and freaked out. As he ran away terrified, he noted that his hiccups were gone. It never occurred to me to wonder just why Dracula would have a huge crucifix hanging on his own wall…

Back then, Saturday morning cartoons were the real thing. Plenty of new characters invented for television happily shared time with the theatrical classics of Bugs Bunny, the Pink Panther, and others. And this was long before the PTA teamed up with Congress to assign the blame for real-life violence to that perpetrated by the gleeful Looney Tunes. These cartoons ran uncensored and unfettered with their glorious imagination and insane humor… and then when the sun went down, those lucky viewers who got to watch "Creature Features" (if their parents weren't controlling the set, or if Carol Burnett, All in the Family, Bob Newhart, and Mary Tyler Moore were in reruns, that is) and see that sense of imagination applied to darker material. And yes, even at that tender age, we were aware of the difference between make-believe and grim reality. We had the war. We had Watergate. And we had the news. The news which would frequently intrude upon our beloved programming just to make sure we never forgot what was really going on out there.

The monsters which populated my crude grade-school drawings liked nothing better than to watch themselves on TV. But my cartoons reflected the frustrating reality that they, too, would have to deal with. The Frankenstein Monster, for instance, settled down to watch one of his appearances on Creature Features, only to be confronted with the typical announcement, "We interrupt this program

Illustration: Stephen R. Bissette

for a Special Report." The pattern continued unabated until the Monster decided to do something about it. So, he walked over to the costume shop and picked up a Western bad guy outfit complete with domino mask and toy gun. Thus equipped, he made his way to the TV station and easily found the technician responsible. And just as the technician started to announce, "We interrupt this program…" yet again, the disguised Monster pulled his toy gun on the malefactor and said, "Stick 'em up!" for the punchline. And no, it never occurred to me that the Frankenstein Monster himself might be frightening enough without the masked bandit disguise. He was just one of the guys and he just wanted to watch his show. Just like us.

No, neither classic cartoons nor classic monsters ever instilled a violent impulse in me, or influenced me to behave in any negative way. Quite the contrary—they made me want to learn more. The monsters, in particular, inspired me to catalog their adventures and seek out as much additional reading material as possible. My problem, of course, was that I was hyper-enthused to share the resulting knowledge with anyone who would listen. So of course, in addition to the expected, "If only you paid as much attention to your schoolwork as you did your monsters," I received plenty of unsolicited counseling from teachers and self-appointed case workers alike; all of whom advised me with varying levels of gentleness and intensity that I had outgrown the monsters and that it was time for me to move on. And I listened. And I listened. (I really had no choice.) But it did no good. By that time, I had discovered horror hosts. I'd seen several different examples by the time Rich Koz hit the airwaves as the Son of Svengoolie as the '70s became the '80s, but Koz (yes, the former Son is still going strong with the classic monsters as Svengoolie himself to this day, and long may he continue to reign) was THE differ-

ence-maker. He gave us monsters, he gave us comedy, and people LOVED watching him. What do you know… it was OKAY to be a monster kid after all!

A lazy Alfred didn't want to bother crossing the study to alert Bruce Wayne to Commissioner Gordon's urgent call in my completely unauthorized Batman parody comics. So, he merely bellowed, "IT'S THE BATPHONE!" for everyone, including Aunt Harriet, to hear. Aunt Harriet then confronted Bruce Wayne with, "So

"Chas, Greg Goodsell, and others with whom I enjoyed camaraderie during that heyday turned me on to many a film I would go on to screen for the program."

YOU'RE Batman!" And… POW! Bruce knocked her out with a single punch on the way to the Batpoles. Later, after Batman (drawn relatively normally) and Robin (beak, wings… you get it) put paid to the Masked Meatball, they passed a public square where, to their horror, Aunt Harriet was standing behind a podium and shouting, "Bruce Wayne is Batman! Bruce

Wayne is Batman!" to a crowd of listeners. So, Batman and Robin grabbed a couple of clubs and managed to knock out each and every person in the public square so that they'd get amnesia and forget the whole thing. It was no more violent than a typical Batman episode (poor King Tut got concussion amnesia so many times that it was amazing that his loaf wasn't simply and permanently bashed in); but yeah, decking Aunt Harriet was a bit more edgy than people had come to expect of me…

Meanwhile, we had no less than SEVEN weekend Creature Feature shows happening, from Friday nights through Sunday afternoons, on three different channels. Conflicts and choices between stations in those pre-VCR days could be troublesome, but it was still horror heaven. People who paid attention to these shows didn't just get the Universal, Hammer, and AIP classics anymore. They got a crash course in horror films from all over the world, and the truly dedicated learned more from the movies that came to them than a typical textbook could provide. They also noticed that a lot of the new arrivals pushed well past the safety/comfort zone to which they had become accustomed…

…but not even the most transgressive late-night TV selections could hold a candle to what was happening on the big screen in the wake of Halloween, Dawn of the Dead, and ALIEN. And eventually, they stopped trying.

It all changed in the 1980s. The classic cartoons disappeared in favor of toy commercials (no, I didn't skip the Transformers movies for being overblown Michael Bay epics—I skipped them because I never watched the original cartoon in the first place, so resentful was I that they, along with He-Man, G.I. Joe, and countless others had removed my beloved Pink Panther, Tom and Jerry, and Popeye from the airwaves!); the home video phenomenon grew exponentially; and the "infomercial"

la Grande Paura

DEBORAH WALLEY · PAUL CARR · DAVID CANNON · VINCENT MARTORANO · JOHN CRAWFORD · MARVIN KAPLAN

REGIA DI THOMAS S. ALDERMAN   EASTMANCOLOR

spelled doom for all late-night local movie programming, hosted or not. After all—who's going to pay someone to host their dusty old movies when all manner of people were willing to pay THEM to advertise their junk all night?

And just how would the horror historians of the future learn their craft without at least one program that brought the movies to THEM on a regular basis?

In my "New Brady Bunch" comics, Sam the butcher was bitten severely on the wrist by a rabid tiger. Terrified of getting rabies shots, Sam chose to put his own hand down on the chopping block and sever it with a meat cleaver. He then screwed a meat hook directly into the bone to serve as his new appendage.

Thanks to my good friend Norm (a disciple of the special makeup techniques showcased by Dick Smith, Rick Baker, Rob Bottin, and Tom Savini), we actually re-created this gruesome fantasy on video. I played Sam with gusto, but Norm did all the rest. I actually kept that hook-hand prosthetic intact throughout the 1980s and used it as my signature as I attempted to

entertain college crowds as demented prop/gore comic "Remo D." Part of Remo's act involved screening any number of hand-removal scenes from his favorite horror movies as an explanation. And Remo D. would cap off his show by screening a full-length horror movie for those who wished to remain in the cantina.

Remo D. wasn't originally intended to be confused with "serious" horror historian, Shane M. Dallmann. He existed in his own world for no nobler purpose than to share horror and monster movies with anyone who cared to listen. Just like his younger self. But when our late, great Deep Red Founder, Chas Balun, welcomed Hand It to Remo into these very pages, he inadvertently gave the game away with the byline on the very first installment. Still, no regrets. As Remo prepared to sign off on what he thought would be his final column, he had finally achieved his goal of appearing on local television as a horror host... and he encouraged his readers to look into the field themselves, and avail themselves of both public access television and the internet.

Remo D.'s Manor of Mayhem spent its first season on the air in 2002 under the delusion that it represented the "last" bastion of television horror hosting (essentially, unless you WERE Svengoolie, you were NOT on broadcast television). I hosted the show with a new look and a new hook since my cantina days, and it was my privilege to bring viewers some of the very films I was raving about in Deep Red (yeah, The Severed Arm is a public domain staple, but I was the only one who had the uncut version). With the stalwart Dr. Montag (Dave Deacon) raising any amount of hell with his fiendish experiments and the loyal Kato, the Black Hornet (Gregg Galdo) defending the unit (not to mention the two of them producing, directing and basically providing us with a SHOW to begin with... I can't possibly overstate

REMO D

"It wasn't long before we discovered that we were only the newest members of an amazing network known as the Horror Host Underground..."

their contributions over the years), Remo showed whatever the hell he wanted to show and also carefully explained exactly why he was bringing these very movies to fresh attention week after week.

And to our delight, it wasn't long before we discovered that we were only the newest members of an amazing network known as the Horror Host Underground. No, monster kid, you were NEVER alone. And you

THE MOST HORRIFYING SYNDICATE OF EVIL IN HISTORY!

Each a master of depravity... Each with a mistress to match!

AMERICAN INTERNATIONAL presents
CHRISTOPHER LEE · LEO GENN
STARRING IN
PSYCHO-CIRCUS

WITH   ANTHONY   HEINZ   EDDI   KLAUS   MARGARET   SUZY   GUEST STARS   CECIL   VICTOR   ALSO STARRING   MAURICE
NEWLANDS · DRACHE · ARENT · KINSKI · LEE · KENDALL · PARKER · MADDERN · KAUFMANN
PRODUCED BY HARRY ALAN TOWERS · DIRECTED BY JOHN MOXEY · SCREENPLAY BY PETER WELBECK · AN AMERICAN INTERNATIONAL RELEASE

didn't have competitors—you had collaborators. A. Ghastlee Ghoul. The Bone Jangler. Halloween Jack. Butch R. Cleaver. Dr. Dreck and Moaner. Undead Johnny. Professor Griffin. Karlos Borloff. Sally, the Zombie Cheerleader. Penny Dreadful. And so, so many others for your discovery. Between guest appearances on set and guest shows airing between our reruns, they were all a huge part of the Manor effect for 16 years and 20 seasons (before we retired the show with honors).

Deep Red was a huge part of the Manor effect, as well. Chas, Greg Goodsell, and others with whom I enjoyed camaraderie during that heyday turned me on to many a film I would go on to screen for the program. Greg even appeared live on set when we ran the Christopher Lee vehicle Circus of Fear ("Where's the soikus! I wanna soikus!"). Far more sobering, however, was the double-tribute we aired when we received the sad news that Chas had departed this realm. For me, it was only half of a two-part shocker; as scarcely a week had passed since the death of my friend Paul Naschy. The Spanish horror king had been a Manor mainstay in his own right (he had given me specific permission to screen any of his films and I ended up running approximately 20 of them over 20 seasons!), of course. Ironically, Chas himself didn't care for Naschy's work much at all (not that he ever discouraged me from promoting it in my Deep Red reviews); but he wound up on the same tribute program in which I removed my hat and hook and simply introduced myself as Shane, and showed the viewers the "many faces of Naschy" painting that I myself had commissioned… from none other than Chas.

Deep Red, in whatever format it may take, remains my "horror hosting" vehicle. And yes, Hand It to Remo is still my "hand removal" vehicle. Remember my earlier reference to the innocent 1960s Batman TV series (and yes, RIP to the great Adam West, as well)? Now we have Gotham as we enjoy an era of unfettered,

ghastly, gruesome and gory goodies on NETWORK TELEVISION, yet. Gotham, to my delight, has had more than a generous share of "Remo D. moments" over the course of its first few seasons. The

Penguin got his henchman Butch nice and relaxed before striking his hand off with a meat cleaver right on camera (yes, just like Sam the Butcher)! In a later episode, the Riddler put the hand of a young villainess known as Tabby into a guillotine contraption and gave that same Butch a chance to save her from that fate. He didn't. (Okay,

she got her hand re-attached in time, but it still came off on camera, so it still counts.) And Jim Gordon just blasted the manual appendage clean off of the crazed Captain Barnes where last we left things… yep—this show is me all over. Tell me again how we're responsible for all the real-life violence and horror in the world?

A disaffected and morbid Archie Andrews finds even his secret life as Super Pimp unfulfilling. As a flesh-eating zombie, Jughead's only good as a bodyguard; and not even Reggie's transformation into a female prostitute can stop his mouth from getting him into lethal trouble. Perhaps only the disembodied brain of Dilton Doiley can unlock…

Oh, who am I kidding? I just got a load of the first season of Riverdale, Archie's been banging Miss Grundy, and the murder mystery hanging over the entire town is solved when the gang winds up watching a snuff video on a computer. Who the hell needs me?

We interrupt this program for a Special Report…

GEORGE A. ROMERO IS DEAD. LONG LIVE GEORGE ROMERO.

A Personal Remembrance

Dennis Daniel

Epiphanies are rare in life. It's not very often that we find ourselves in a place or situation that is life-changing and unforgettable. Three of my greatest were tied to George A. Romero.

Like every writer in this mag—as well as many more who write about the horror film genre—there's no end to the literature that relates to how magnificent an achievement Night of the Living Dead was, and is. I need not add anything more to that, or comment on Romero's other Dead films. Groundbreaking. Original. Eternal. Classic. 'Nuff said.

What I felt when I heard of his passing was more personal. I met the man. We spoke at length more than once. I watched him work. Incredible. With your kind indulgence, I'd like to share some personal memories with you.

EPIPHANY #1:

My first G.A.R. encounter was in 1985. I was working at WBAB, a rock station in Babylon, Long Island. We were involved with a promotion that was heaven on earth for me. Tickets were being given out to the world premiere of Day of the Dead in NYC. I was hosting the event. Can you imagine? There was once a time when no one really knew if there would ever be a sequel to Dawn of the Dead.

There had been months of great reporting from the Day of the Dead set in Fangoria, and in other publications. Fans were well aware of the film, thanks to the various stills and images (no internet then, of course) that came our way. One of the most exciting aspects of it all was the astonishing make-up effects by the great Tom Savini, who was at his absolute apex as the FX master. Oh, it was an exciting time, to

be sure. I went to the premiere dressed as a zombie. We also had tickets to the afterparty at a cool NYC nightclub called Arena.

What happened at this premiere would never happen again.

The audience was filled to the rafters with RABID FANS. George was in attendance, as well as Tom Savini, the cast, and the producers. I was introduced to George by his PR person, and he was as gracious and nice a fellow as I had always heard. He laughed at my zombie-ness. We chatted for a bit about what he went through to make the film, and about his expectations for it. Mind you, this was several years before I even began writing about the genre.

The time came for the film to start, and—right away—the whooping and hollering and complete immersion of the crowd into the film was phenomenal. When we first

74

saw Dr. Tongue (based on a mold of Savini himself!), the place went apeshit! And rightfully so. From that moment on, with every special effect, people just wailed with delight! I am talking about EVERY SINGLE EFFECT! Because they were all groundbreaking!!! The guts spilling out of the zombie getting off the slab! CROWD: "WOOOOW! OH, MY GOD!" The corpse on the gurney with just his brain exposed. CROWD: "HOLY SHIT!" The machete chopping off the infected arm. "AHHHH-HHHH!!!" And on and on.

Can you imagine? It was truly a communal experience... a gathering of the tribes, all possessed of one mind. (You think anything like this happens these days with CGI? Forget it! All FX are taken for granted these days! The millennials think it's all rote. Sigh.)

To this day, I can't watch Day of the Dead without hearing the crowd roar with every effect. It must have made Savini and Romero so happy to hear all that chaos of amazement.

At the afterparty, I met all the principles again. I'll never forget when I met Terry Alexander and discovered his Jamaican accent was NOT his real voice. He laughed at me and said, loudly, "Fooled you, mon!" It was beyond a dream come true in every way.

EPIPHANY #2:

Fast forward to 1989. Thanks to my good pal Roy Frumkes, we were on the set of Two Evil Eyes in (where else?) Pittsburgh. He had asked me along to take stills for his continuing Document of the Dead project. He was doing new interviews with George. By then, I was writing for Deep Red, and my assignment was to interview George on video for an upcoming FantaCon show... and to visit Savini at his make-up shop and home (in order to talk about Two Evil Eyes and his plans for directing the remake of Night of the Living Dead). When we got

to the set, George was directing the scene where the triangular obelisk falls straight into Ramy Zada's chest. It was being done by holding the prop above him with vacuum suction. It had to fall EXACTLY on the fake Ramy chest prosthetic attached to his torso. Ramy had to BE THERE, in a very uncomfortable position, hoping that it landed properly... which it was having a hard time doing. George was directing the scene, playing with a yo-yo... which he called his "smoking substitute." Later, I went to Tom's shop and interviewed him at his house and... how cool is this... as he drove me to the airport! (Yes, TOM drove me!) We had become pals by then. I had done that Deep Red interview [Deep Red volume 1, number 3 — ed.] with him and he was very pleased with it. All of this footage is available on the EXTRAS section of the Two Evil Eyes DVD and Blu-ray. The photo of me (in my Deep Red T-shirt) and George was taken on the set. We took time to chat after the scene was done, and he was just wonderful! No ego. Totally genu-

ine and REAL. An amazing man.

EPIPHANY #3:

Fast forward again. A few months later, I was in Washington, Pennsylvania on the set of the Night of the Living Dead remake. I got to be in the flesh-eating scene! You see me quite clearly. Tom was kind enough to invite me to be in the film. Once again, there was George on the set. He remembered me (honest!), and we hung out for quite a while talking about the state of the genre, and his happiness that the film would put the copyright back with all the principles. He was also so excited about Tom directing, and was very pleased with the rewrite that he did on the script. I can't begin to tell you what it was like being on this set. Sitting on the sidelines and watching hundreds of zombies walking by the camera. Being directed by Tom in my scenes. Seeing George right there next to him! MIND BLOWING (or as dear Chas would say... CHUNK BLOWING) in every way.

So, when George passed, it felt personal.

I have also had the joy of hanging out with many of the actors from the "first" Dead trilogy. You can see what that was like in Roy Frumkes' The Definitive Document of the Dead. I actually picked up Judith O'Dea and drove her to the interview we did at Roy's party. How cool is that? At FantaCon 2013, my wife Lynda and I got to hang with the NOTLD cast! The dead really do NEVER STAY DEAD.

I love all the Dead films George did! Each one is a gift. Look at what our culture has done with zombies. He was the starting point. There will never be another one like him, nor will there ever be the kind of times that he created in. His legacy is sealed with blood and will forever live on... just like his living dead.

God bless you, George.
And thanks.

THE OTHER DEAD TRILOGY

Mike Hunchback

George Romero is gone, but he will never be forgotten. His cinematic achievements are the stuff of legend, but the mindset behind them was even more exceptional. The original Dead trilogy—Night of the Living Dead (1968), Dawn of the Dead (1978), and Day of the Dead (1985)—fought a long, hard battle to achieve the status they hold today. We think of these films as mainstream now, and rightfully so. NOTLD is part of the Museum of Modern Art's permanent library, an American classic. But when critic Roger Ebert saw the film on its original 1968 theatrical run, all he could think about was how unfair it was that the unknowing kids in the audience had been lured into such a disgusting movie. In his infamously mixed-up original review for Night of the Living Dead, he wrote:

"This was ghouls eating people up—and you could actually see what they were eating. This was little girls killing their mothers. This was being set on fire. Worst of all, even the hero got killed." [Jeez, Roger, spoiler alert!]

Yes, it's true. At different times, these

"I always wanted to see how the other side lives..."
— *Cholo (John Leguizamo), Land of the Dead*

films were panned, banned, and lambasted. But they wouldn't go away, eventually becoming part of the American cultural

lexicon as much as Poe's The Raven, or Universal monster movies. Responsible for their longevity was Romero's profound original concept: commenting on contemporary social issues through horror and extreme, yet unseen gore. This concept operates at full-force in the original Dead trilogy; the Vietnam War, consumerism, and authority figures are among the prime targets that the writer/director gutted with his sly, deeply idealistic visions. Romero often talked about the 1960s hippie movement and how its goal of spreading peace and love had failed, ultimately affecting only a fraction of the change they had wanted. Living during those heady times and believing in his heart that the Love Generation was going to make a difference, Romero ended up being one of many disillusioned idealists. But instead of going the direction that most did (abandoning hope for world peace altogether and trading it in for good ol' fashioned selfishness and greed), a deeply ingrained rage grew in him. Romero harnessed this rage and used it to tell confrontational, moralistic stories in a way that has drastically expanded the language of filmmaking and art in general. Before industrial music, heavy metal, or punk rock were utilizing extreme confrontational aspects, before experimental art films grew a pair, Romero was the guy who figured out that if you could freak your audience out hard enough, you just might be able to get them to think. Maybe even change their minds… It's a debt that could never be repaid. Night of the Living Dead changed the world, period.

Yet, after 1985's Day of the Dead, the Dead trilogy was just that—dead. Hope of Romero doing another entry faded into the long years. But when the new millennium came, a shocking wave of sequels and remakes was unleashed, and the marketability of another Dead flick became very real. In 2005, with Romero at age 65, Land of the Dead was released. With a respectable regularity Romero and a variety of encouraging producers followed with Diary of the Dead in 2007 and Survival of the Dead in 2009.

So… What of Romero's other Dead trilogy? Due to the intense disapproval of some fans and lack of mainstream recognition, the films are rarely discussed seriously. For many, it's hard to imagine further Dead films ever matching the bold combination of searing dramatic satire and sublime gut-munching found in the original Dead trilogy. At the time, some fans wondered if Romero should even go there, worried it could somehow spoil the glory of his previous unparalleled achievements.

Five long years had passed since Romero's underrated Bruiser when it was announced that he was making Land of the Dead, a bonafide canonical entry in his Dead series. Perhaps the most popular of the other Dead trilogy films, Land of the Dead's greatest success is that it isn't another Dead film, it's a new Dead film, dealing with its own contemporary issues and fully embodying Romero's patented fevered blend of satire and terror. Made just a few years after 9/11, it's a brutal critique of its era's authoritarian leanings, fueled by lied-to masses via promises of safety and

the false glimmer of hope that the poor can become rich one day.

Land's scope is huge, exploring a layered, multi-faceted society, complete with

"What of Romero's other Dead trilogy? Due to the intense disapproval of some fans and lack of mainstream recognition, the films are rarely discussed seriously."

its own class system, leaders, followers and philosophies. Dennis Hopper plays Kaufman, the ultimate political satire villain (an echo of then-Secretary of Defense Donald Rumsfeld), who's cockily trying to maintain an extravagant lifestyle for himself and other wealthy survivors in a high-rise complex called Fiddler's Green, which is only possible through the control and exploitation of the masses of poor living outside the heavily secured building. Noble nice-guy Riley Denbo (Simon Baker) is part of a roving militarized troop that does jobs for Kaufman in a beastly armed vehicle named Dead Reckoning; he works with Cholo DeMora (John Leguizamo), a moral-questioning street smart tough guy, and a faithful sharpshooting burn victim, Charlie (Robert Joy).

The film prophesizes a harrowingly prescient concept: steel cage zombie death matches, over which unseemly residents of the underworld bet. Riley learns that zombie vs. zombie fights aren't enough anymore when he witnesses Slack (Asia Argento in a classic Romero strong female protagonist role) get tossed in to the cage. Riley rescues her, but this unfortunately leads to himself, Charlie, and Slack getting entrenched in Kaufman's power-hungry madness.

Land is also awesomely gory, and it's chock full of zombies. Their leader is Big Daddy: the lone ghoul at the forefront of undead evolution. It's a fantastic notion that lies at the heart of the other Dead trilogy. Is it possible? Could these ferocious, feral creatures one day organize out of sheer evolutionary will?

Land's $15 million plus budget didn't earn a huge return. Yet, due to Romero's interest in a sequel and willingness to do it cheaply, a follow-up was announced. Diary of The Dead sees Romero directing with the brazen confidence of a college student. Forced to work within a two-million-dollar budget, Romero landed on a POV/found footage format for Diary. Some groaned at the news—anyone would admit it's become a tired trope. But, after Cannibal Holocaust and before The Blair Witch Project, John McNaughton filmed a scene for his Henry: Portrait of a Serial Killer that I say forever proves the format's potential, wherein Henry and his cohort Otis amateurishly videotape themselves as they invade a home and murder the average suburban family that lives there, later watching their inhuman crime for kicks on their new VCR. It's a firing-at-all-pistons assault on the audience, who are immediately able to identify with the victims' helplessness. I hoped that this was the direction Romero would go in with Diary…

Diary of the Dead is a POV/found footage movie by way of a perfect storm of first-person footage and surveillance video, shot and compiled by a rogue college film crew. While filming an embarrassingly cheesy horror film in the woods, they hear a news report about rioting and mass murder, only to find out soon after that it's actually the zombie apocalypse. The group's director Jason (Joshua Close) leads the crew and their alcoholic teacher/comic relief Mr. Wentworth (Andrew Maxwell) on

a disastrous road-trip to find his girlfriend Debra (Michelle Morgan), while also trying to avoid being eaten alive. Along the way they encounter a colorful array of characters, including a tough-as-nails mute Amish farmer (character actor R.D. Reid). Class and racial tensions are addressed when they meet an armed, gang-like squad lead by "Stranger" (Martin Roach). Alan Van Sprang from Land shows up again as Colonel, robbing the kids blind at government-issued gunpoint.

Sometime after Land was completed, Romero made the choice to overlook a few details and use the character(s) of Brubaker/Colonel/Sarge (all Van Sprang) as a through line, also re-arranging the time line. Diary is at the beginning of the outbreak in the way Night of the Living Dead was, before the shopping mall bunkers and isolated army bases. It's an interesting idea, and gives the three films some weight when considering Van Sprang's dynamic arc.

After getting Debra and losing several members, the remainders of the crew hole up in a large, seemingly safe mansion, only to succumb to temptations of mistrust, which leads to Debra being the lone survivor—Diary is her edit of this footage, with her narration. As she ponders some video for potential inclusion, she shudders as she watches some gun crazy hicks use zombies for target practice, asking a question that will prove relevant in the next installment: "Are we worth saving?"

This is Romero's message in Diary, but it's sadly undersold. Explained to the audience, the point falls flat. If the audience was forced to turn away from the screen like the original audience for Dawn was however, it may have registered. Dawn is the template for over-the-top gorefests: bodies were torn apart, machetes chopped heads like melons, intestines were chomped down on like hot dogs, and audiences were stunned—Romero had revolutionarily used hyper-violence to drive home his message on consumerism. Diary should have updated this for the post-internet era, with a sensibility of the

kinds of sadistic violence one can access online in seconds. Diary toys with the idea that technology has fueled our insatiable desire to film catastrophe, but it's not really proven. Instead of using found footage for its fear appeal to the same numbing degree that Dawn used gut-munching, it's scaled back to the gore we might expect from a

modern zombie flick. Exploring the levels of perversion and depravity that humans who capture zombies for amusement would go to may have been the last uncharted territory that zombie movies had, and while the idea of Diary exists upon this notion, it doesn't feel like it's what the film is really about. This problematic factor of Diary is its weakest link—had the film truly explored the kinds of sickness we might see uploading internet videos in the years after a zombie outbreak, I think it could have been the crown jewel in Romero's career.

All of that said, I often wonder how Diary of the Dead will age. Regardless of what I think of Diary's quality as a fear film, it remains ambitious and brave, something that future film historians will likely commend Romero for. He may have complained about his inability to fund dream projects in these later years, but here's a guy pushing seventy who still seriously had the fire burning in him. Not only did he want to do something as crazy as a found footage zombie feature, but he was also willing to risk his most commercial property to do so. Rare is the case where a movie's aspirations weigh so heavily upon its legacy. Like Diary or hate it, it stands as further proof of Romero's eternal energy and guts.

The last film in the series' timeline, Survival of the Dead, takes place when even the last bastions of "society" like Fiddler's Green have fallen. There are no cities of any kind anymore, all that's left are sparsely populated small-scale infrastructures. One such is Plum Island, off the coast of Delaware, where two long-battling families try to stay alive while still clinging to their hatred of each other. It's Romero's return to the kind of classical Western format that had captured his imagination as a kid: Survival's Muldoons/O'Flynns blood feud is pure Hatfields/McCoys, cut from the same cloth as an old John Wayne film. Alan Van Sprang's "Sarge" Crockett gets caught up in the middle of this dispute, originally believing the isolated island could become a safe home to his rogue troop.

At first, the origins of the families' mysterious dispute aren't questioned, the issue of the day having shifted to undead relations. The O'Flynns want all zombies destroyed, but the Muldoons think this task is impossible, opting to devote their efforts to finding a way to co-exist peacefully with ghouls. The Muldoons' patriarch Seamus (Richard Fitzpatrick) has been experimenting with feeding zombies animal flesh, working toward a generation of undead that need not threaten humanity. But Patrick O'Flynn (Kenneth Welsh) mixes arrogance with vengeance, and uses this disagreement to fuel the deep hatred he has for the Muldoons. In the classic Romero mold, these are people who would likely survive, if only they could find a way to live together.

When looked at as a whole, the other Dead trilogy hits hard on its best theme: the inevitable evolution of zombies from mere flesh-eating creatures to functioning beings in their own societies, and it's best handled in Survival. The constant theme of all the Dead films—can humans ever find a way to survive together in extreme crisis, and does their inability to do so make them equally as monstrous as their undead foes?—is built up to a poetic conclusion also, one worthy of closing the series. In Night of the Living Dead we realize that, try as you might to live righteously, the outside force of society's shortcomings will always be ready and strong enough to ruin you in the blink of an eye. The furthering of the concept that we learn in Survival is especially excellent: zombies can in fact evolve to exist without requiring the consumption of human meat, but so long as the living are around the bloodshed isn't going to stop. It's an uncompromisingly dark, exceptionally raw notion... Zombies aren't the monsters. We are.

Survival's weak point is one also found in Diary, one that's become more digestible over time: CGI gore simply doesn't compare to practical effects. The visceral nastiness that concludes Day of the Dead, where the villains are literally ripped apart, still screaming as their entrails are torn out by a fiendish flesh-chomping sea of the undead, will forever be the height of zombie gore, and Survival's frequency of digital gore can be distracting. But let's not kid ourselves— the use of computer effects allowed Romero to make three more Dead films, tell three more stories. And we're better off for it.

Romero gave his undead a glorious

birth—the intensity of students rioting against armed cops and explosive Vietnam protests somehow distilled into drive-in movie framework. Most other filmmakers would have left it at that, more concerned with maintaining a legacy than with the potential of the here and now. For him to use this other Dead trilogy to tell us that a planet's worth of gut-munchers, who his heroes have been fighting forever, can actually be more civilized than the living deserves considerable praise.

Sure, sequels and remakes can sting, but I look at it this way: if there's ever an argument that boils down to should George fucking Romero make films or not make films, I go with "make films" every time. The truth is that Land of the Dead, Diary of the Dead, and Survival of the Dead don't need to be as good as their predecessors. Period. They're different films, from a different era. From the couch, sure, it's easy to pick apart the clunky elements in movies. But realistically, the process of making them is so vastly complex that to simply bash a film by someone like Romero is a generally uninteresting and bitter game to play. We need to talk about his films the

way we might talk about the films of say, Orson Welles or Fellini. Artists whose bodies of work are so extremely multi-faceted that "lesser" films become potentially significant for many varieties of reasons. Academics and film geeks alike can read into these filmographies and find their own meanings, over and over. Playing favorites is a useless exercise here.

George Romero, more than any other filmmaker, is the prime example of horror's relationship with independence. "I'm not a Hollywood guy," Romero said with a smile in interviews. He, who gave us Night of the Living Dead, was also an extremely outspoken critic of the system, seeing it as an enemy of creativity. "Do you own the thing," "never sell out," "don't let the bastards grind you down"... This attitude is at the core of who we are as horror fans. Everything about us celebrates rebellion. Personal integrity and independence are basically accepted as the norm for us. Since the '60s, the overwhelming majority of the great horror films have not been products of Hollywood. Since NOTLD, horror fans generally don't accept major studio fodder as the real deal. We're nobody's pushovers, man, and Romero's character fits directly into that. In a way, you could say that horror gets its misery from Poe, its romance from Dracula and its rebellion from George Romero.

It's in this respect that I think we need this return of Deep Red. When Chas Balun did Deep Red originally, he took Romero's lesson on rebellion and ran with it. At a time when people would laugh at you for calling a bloody horror movie a valid work of art, Chas used his zine to establish a sense of community among misanthrope gorehounds, while film critics and the general public alike were regulating films like Romero's to the genre ghetto. Originally, people tried to condemn Romero for his rebelliousness, but instead he proudly turned it into his legacy. We, too, as gorehounds, as rebels, as outsiders, should be proud— and maniacally happy—to wear our hearts on our bloody sleeves... After all: isn't that what Chas—and George—would have done?

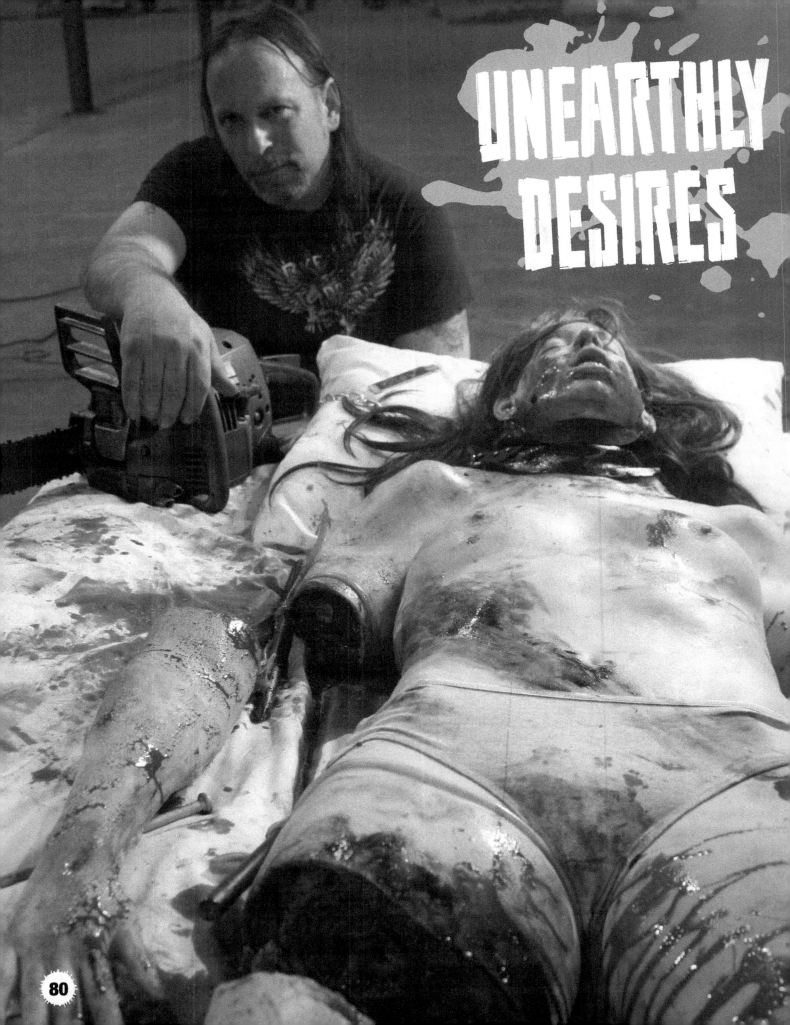

UNEARTHLY DESIRES

Stephen Biro Spills His Guts!

John Szpunar

The point that I'm about to make has been proven time and time again. For some strange reason, the people responsible for directing the most notorious films in the history of modern horror cinema have turned out to be some of the friendliest people I've ever met. Four cases immediately spring to mind: Jörg Buttgereit, director of the infamous Nekromantik, is one of the sweetest people that I've ever had the pleasure of calling a friend. Buddy Giovinazzo, the director of Combat Shock, is one of the nicest guys on the face of the planet. Fred Vogel (of August Underground fame) is a calm, soft-spoken gent. And then, there's this Stephen Biro guy.

Stephen Biro is the president of Unearthed Films, and the director of American Guinea Pig: Bouquet of Guts and Gore and American Guinea Pig: The Song of Solomon. Gruesome, terrifying, disgusting, and nerve-shattering are just four adjectives that you could use to describe his films. You could also add the words thoughtful, uncompromising, methodical, and spiritual to the mix. To beat an old cliché to death, his films make me anxious and uneasy. They make me think. They also gross me the FUCK out. And that, my friends, is no easy feat!

And, what do you know? Stephen Biro is also one hell of a gracious gore-meister! Deep Red sat down for a long chat with the man shortly before The Song of Solomon premiered at the 2017 Sitges Film Festival in Spain. Pull up a chair, and listen in...

DEEP RED: When I first heard about Bouquet of Guts and Gore, I knew that it was a movie that I needed to see. At the same time, I was very afraid of what I was going to see. The movie didn't disappoint! The levels of dread that I felt during the experience were almost unbearable. Was this your intent?

STEPHEN BIRO: Of course! We purposely dragged out the beginning a little to make the viewer uneasy 'cause once it

starts going... it doesn't really stop until the end. Working with Kristian Day and Jimmy ScreamerClauz for the music helped a lot 'cause we wanted this industrial noise dread behind the devastation you were watching on screen. Guess it worked.

RED: What made you want to tackle an "American" approach to the original Guinea Pig series?

SB: I always loved the Guinea Pig series... it sort of shows. I wanted to start the series up again, and it took forever to get the rights. When the head owner of the Japanese company was retiring, he said, "Fuck it, here you go." It's sort of funny—when we started Unearthed Films, I wanted to make a splash and show that we were the extreme gore label, so we went with Flowers of Flesh and Blood as the first release. When I was in the position to start directing and producing movies, it was only fitting that I direct the first film. It fell into place that it is the prequel to Flowers of Flesh and Blood.

RED: Let's back up for a second. When did you first become interested in horror?

SB: I've been a horror fan since I was five years old. Used to buy Creepy magazine back in the day. Came across the first issue of Fangoria at a convenience store. What really helped was that my stepdad stole a VHS player from Sears. He worked as a mechanical engineer for them back in 1981. The things were like three grand back in the day, and no one had them at the time. The video store only had 70 VHS copies to rent since it was so brand new. So, it was easy to go through movies and the parents would rent Andy Warhol's Frankenstein, Evil Dead, and such when I was in the sixth grade. It also helped that my mom would put a rubber monster under my pillow instead of a quarter when the tooth fairy came.

RED: How did your tastes change as you grew older?

SB: Got more violent, wanted more intensity with my horror films. When I finally got my hands on Cannibal Holocaust and Nekromantik, it was heaven. The '80s helped with some off-the-wall films. It was a great time to be a horror fan since so many filmmakers were actually making good money and horror films were watched by everyone. The international horror films really began to get more violent, so that was a major plus for me.

RED: Before starting Unearthed Films, you worked in the comic book field. What was that experience like?

SB: It was fun. Sort of like playing the stock market. I specialized in the gore/horror comics like Faust and Lady Death. I read everything under the sun back in those days. I got out right when the industry imploded and CGC [grading] sort of killed it. I always warned people that the Beanie Baby is not going to be worth anything later, so sell it when you can.

RED: You knew Chas. Balun back in the day. Any memories of him that you'd like to share?

SB: He knew me as a fan. He was a great individual who cared about his fans, and we talked here or there on the phone. He saw me go from a fan to opening Video Mayhem of Florida, and then to Unearthed Films. I had him write an essay on the GP films and what happened with the Charlie Sheen fiasco. It's on the DVD of Flowers of Flesh and Blood. I was trying to get a couple of films made in the early 2000s, and Chas. sent me the script for A Deeper Red. He actually sent me the original. Needless to say, production didn't get off the ground.

RED: You were involved in the bootleg tape scene of the 1990s. How did this lead to your involvement in the Guinea Pig films from Japan?

SB: Funny story. I got hit by the company handling the Guinea Pig films for international through Video Mayhem of Florida. It

was right when I was shutting it down. The world got smaller due to the internet, and films were getting real releases on DVD, so I opened a cult video store when I got the copyright infringement notice. Instead of just taking them down, I called them. They were quite surprised. They offered to sell me the films, since I had a whole history page on my site about them. I countered offered with, "Let's start a company together," and they balked. They called me a month later with a lower price, and I offered the same deal. They called me back another month later, and then...

RED: Unearthed Films was born…

SB: Yes, it was. We started with a huge Japanese flavor with the Guinea Pig films and then released Evil Dead Trap 2, Junk, and Boy Meets Girl. Contacted Nacho Cerdà for Aftermath.

RED: Back to Bouquet of Guts and Gore. How did you come up with the idea for the film?

SB: At the beginning of Flowers of Flesh and Blood, it states that Hideshi Hino received an 8mm snuff film in the mail and that Flowers is his recreation of it for Japanese sensibilities. This gave me the wonderful idea—to make the snuff film he watched—and Bouquet of Guts and Gore was born. If you pay attention, we used '80s style clothes and equipment to make it. Since Flowers was made in '86, we figured we would go with the '84 aesthetic. Super 8mm and VHS camcorder. When fans figure this out... or if I let them know, they usually have a deeper appreciation for the film. It's not a remake, reboot, or a sequel. It's the prequel that actually fits perfectly, since they talk about this film at the beginning of Flowers.

RED: Let's talk about FX artist Marcus

Koch. His work is AMAZING.

SB: I've known Marcus for, shit, close to two decades now. We're very good friends; some may even say best friends.

RED: How did you meet him?

SB: His story is, he came into my comic book store and I told him, "Your first mov-

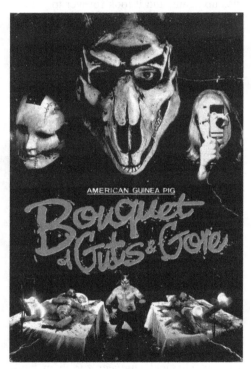

ie sucks." I don't believe it, 'cause I never saw Rot (1999) back in those days. Why would I tell someone their movie sucks if I never saw it? I think he has me mistaken, but who knows? It's sort of funny now, though...

RED: What about Scott Gabbey?

SB: I've known him since 2000. He's such a good friend; we met at the horror conventions in Florida. He's a great guy.

RED: His presence as the Director in Guts and Gore really brings something

to it. Along those lines, how did you meet Jim VanBebber?

SB: I lived in a small town called Crystal River in Florida, and won't ya know it, his mother lived there. He moved in to help take care of her. I got a call from Gabbey and he said, "Dude, you will never guess who just moved into your town." I'm like, "Who?" "James VanBebber." I'm like, "What? I'm the horror guy in this town. [Laughs] Needless to say, [this led to] a lot of drunken shenanigans, and we worked on Gator Green together.

RED: How did you go about casting Bouquet of Guts and Gore?

SB: [There is] a tight group of horror people around Tampa Bay, and if you're going to shoot on film, VanBebber is the only choice for 8mm. And I wanted him to play the Editor in the film. The rest fell into place. To be honest, we had some new talent, so I drugged the women at the very beginning. Everyone else wore masks—if we needed ADR, we could fix their performances. Luckily, we didn't have to. Tampa is a weird place for underground horror. Tons of people making it, but how many do you hear about?

RED: How difficult was it to get the project going?

SB: Not very. I was just finalizing my divorce to my second wife, so I had a little bit of cash. I had also just sold a screenplay to a total nutter called Bubba the Redneck Werewolf. Once you have the cash, it's easy to make a film if you have the time to actually do it. Since I already had a great team with Scott, Marcus, and VanBebber, it pretty much fell into place.

RED: What kind of budget did you have?

SB: I'll be honest—15 grand. Marcus knew this would be a calling card for him, so he busted his ass. I learned a lot of FX through him, since we were roommates at the time. Everyone got paid, everyone was happy. It was a whirlwind of shooting. Three days in a huge warehouse and two days in a friend's house that was being foreclosed on by Bank of America. We left the gore soaked beds in the house as a nice fuck you to the bank. Those beds weighed like 300 pounds each; they were magic beds that Marcus and I built to hide the actresses in.

RED: The Last House on Dead End Street must have a strong influence on the film...

SB: Actually, not at all! It was all a happy coincidence.

RED: No shit? That's great!

SB: Shooting on 8mm film gave it a look that screamed Last House. We didn't notice it because the dailies we were seeing were straight from the VHS camcorder. So, we didn't know until after the 8mm film was developed and sent back to us. When we watched it, it was like, holy fuck... this looks like Last House on Dead End Street! I don't mind people thinking we did it on purpose. It's an accident that we don't mind at all.

RED: What was the initial reaction to the film like?

SB: Shock, awe, and happiness. We thought we were going to get a lot of flak for it once the first round of announcements came out. But once we announced Jim, Marcus, Scott, and such, peoples' interest was piqued. They were like, "Okay... maybe they can pull it off." We have gotten a little bit of bullshit from people [because it was all] practical FX. So many people are used to the CGI shitfests that a few people complained about the FX work. But the gorehounds... they loved it.

RED: Were you happy with the result?

SB: I was thrilled. I had a lot of people tell me, "Dude, this is your first film and your taking on a gore classic. You must be nervous." I was never nervous—I had the best team I could assemble in Florida. The first

time we watched it after its completion, everyone was like, "Fuck... we did it."

RED: Marcus directed the second film in the series, Bloodshock...

SB: Yes. It was a natural progression, since he's a talented filmmaker and he busted his ass on the gore FX for Bouquet. We joke how we will switch back and forth between

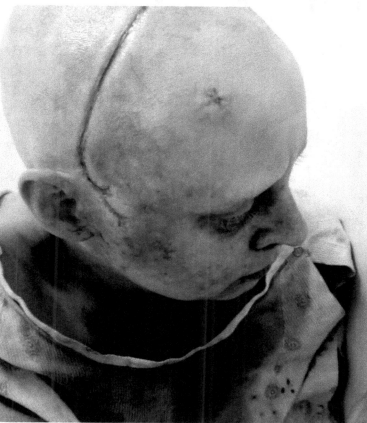

"There is a tight group of horror people around Tampa Bay, and if you're going to shoot on film, VanBebber is the only choice for 8mm."

each movie. I have some other very well-known horror directors lined up, but they [sometimes] drop out due to scheduling and such. So, Marcus may end up directing the next one called The Growing Woman.

RED: How did the process of writing the script for Bloodshock film differ from Bouquet of Guts and Gore?

SB: Bouquet had an actual screenplay. Bloodshock was a nine-page treatment that I wrote. Marcus likes to direct organical-

ly. He loved the idea behind Bloodshock. Writing Bloodshock was more of a spurt of ideas and violence while Bouquet was more methodical in nature with the tortures and snuff crew.

RED: How long did it take for you to write it?

SB: Bouquet took me eight days, Bloodshock, three. I had Bloodshock more planned in my head, while Bouquet is the prequel to Flowers of Flesh and Blood. I had to have more references in it, while Bloodshock came out in a torrent of emotion that leads two people who love each other down a roller-coaster into mutilation.

RED: How did Dan Ellis and the other actors come to be cast?

SB: That was Marcus's doing. He always wanted to work with Dan, so I flew him in along with Lillian McKinley. Marcus knew Andy Winton, who played the Doctor, and he has a specific look about him. I'm glad he joined the AGP family. I knew Gene Palubicki from Angel Corpse for over a decade, and he was up for it. Alberto Giovanelli is a good friend, so we had him play the other orderly. All were amazing on set.

RED: Whose decision was it to shoot in black and white, with the jarring use of color?

SB: Marcus came up with that idea while he was editing. Something clicked for him, and I was like, "But the blood and gore!" Needless to say, when we watched it together, it made the ending so much more beautiful that we were like, "YES!"

RED: Was it difficult for Marcus to direct while also providing the FX?

SB: He had his right-hand girl, Cat Bernier on set, and she was amazing. We also did a lot of the close-ups with the gore FX later. So, Marcus had plenty of time after the initial shooting to make things exactly the way he wanted them.

RED: How did the fan reaction to Bloodshock differ from Bouquet of Guts and Gore?

SB: Two totally different trains of thought. Fans love both, and look at them completely differently. Some were expecting another Bouquet and were pleasantly surprised when it pulled the deep emotion I was going for with the story. Reaction was wonderful for both films.

RED: How did the surprise showing of American Guinea Pig: Sacrifice come about?

SB: Well, Solomon wasn't ready yet, and since Sacrifice was a secret and totally finished, Texas Frightmare was all for it. It was a secret screening—no one knew about Sacrifice yet, and I figured it would be an amazing way to not only get the word out, but to take fans totally by surprise.

RED: What was the audience reaction to that?

SB: Shocked, surprised, and grossed out. People were expecting an exorcism film. Instead, they got our version of He Never Dies, with a guy ripping himself apart in his bathroom. Poison Rouge did an amazing job directing it in Italy. Needless to say, it was a big hit.

RED: How did she get involved?

SB: Domiziano Christopharo was producing it. He contacted me, and it went from there. He and Poison are quite the pair. She doesn't speak any English, so Christopharo was my guy.

RED: It was very cool that a woman directed the film…

SB: People were not expecting it. I may have ruffled a few feathers of other female directors since this was Poison's first fea-

ture film—it came out of the blue. I am happy to say that this is the most extreme horror film ever made by a woman.

RED: You seem to be exploring differ-

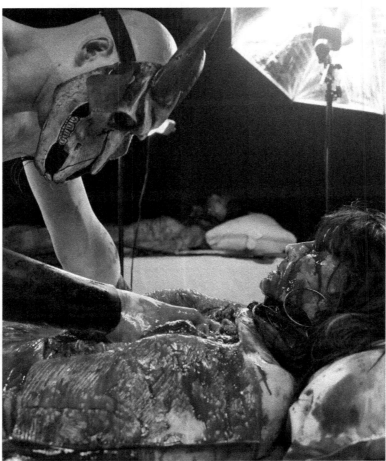

"People were expecting an exorcism film. Instead, they got our version of He Never Dies with a guy ripping himself apart in his bathroom."

ent ways of telling a story as the series progresses…

SB: Oh yeah, just like the original Guinea Pig series. It went from pure torture porn into a sad yet gripping tale of a man's slow turn into insanity with Mermaid in a Manhole. He Never Dies went a bit goofy, and Android was a Sci-Fi gore film. Devil Doctor Woman was even goofier than He Never Dies. The idea is that it's an extreme gore series, and I think we will always try to keep fans on their toes and give them something different yet shocking and revolting

at the same time.

RED: With that in mind, do you consider Song of Solomon to be a departure from the Guinea Pig aesthetic?

SB: Well, it's not torture porn if that's what you mean. But then again, I had it planned after shooting Bouquet. It was supposed to be the last in the series, but other directors' scheduling conflicts arose, and we had this one ready in the wings. So… we went for it. It's an American Guinea Pig film for sure, but totally different.

RED: What made you want to tackle the demonic possession genre?

SB: I'm still amazed at the simple fact that no one has made an exorcism film that didn't pull any punches and went for the gore… and not just rip off The Exorcist.

RED: That's true…

SB: I love possession films, but no one has ever made one that actually sticks out or even comes close to The Exorcist. Same with shark movies like Jaws. It's the reason they are classics. I know a lot about the Catholic exorcism rituals, and no one has ever bothered to do any research about what really happens.

RED: You're throwing new light on the subject.

SB: Yeah. And watching it now, it's as if The Exorcist meets The Evil Dead, in a way. Once it goes off the chain, it just doesn't stop.

RED: In what ways does it differ from the other films in the series?

SB: Besides the budget? I'm still a new filmmaker. Still learning a lot, but I had good teachers. James VanBebber and Mar-

"It went from pure torture porn into a sad yet gripping tale of a man's slow turn into insanity with Mermaid in a Manhole."

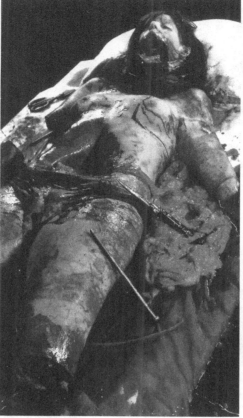

cus Koch taught me a lot, but it was on-set teaching. Learned a lot shooting Gator Green with Jim, and with Bouquet, I was like, "Lets fucking do this!" I bought all the props, had masks made, found the actors, and worked with Marcus on the FX. It taught me a lot, so with Solomon, I got to take all that I had learned, and I ramped up the intensity. I got to hire better actors, but brought along Andy and Gene from Bloodshock. I had my go-to-guy VanBebber, who was actually excited to play a priest. I brought back Scott Gabbey from Bouquet, and it was off to the races! I got to tell more of a story that leads up to the major gore pieces.

"How could I not work with him? It also ramped up the excitement for the gorehounds. Putting Marcus and Jerami on set together... people know it's going to be a bloodbath."

RED: How did your approach to directing differ from the work that you did on Bouquet of Guts and Gore?

SB: Bouquet was an extreme learning process. I just jumped into the deep end, not knowing how to swim. I mean, who is crazy enough to take on a classic gore series like Guinea Pig? With Solomon, it was more deliberate, more nuanced, and I leaned on

my cast, crew, DP, and my FX team more. I was very lucky Jessica Cameron took the role as Mary in Solomon. I had a lot of actresses read the treatment or script and bow out so fast, my head spun. Jessica also helped a lot with the other actors. It was sort of funny, come to think about it. With Solomon, I had actually five other directors working on the film, and everyone worked together; there was no ego clash.

RED: How did you hook up with Jerami Cruise from ToeTag EFX?

SB: Marcus told me to talk to him. It was a natural progression. How could I not work with him? It also ramped up the excitement for the gorehounds. Putting Marcus and Jerami on set together... people know it's going to be a bloodbath.

RED: Sounds great! A clichéd question, but... what's next for you and Unearthed?

SB: Were announcing The Unearthed Classic Lineup, and working on more AGP films. Working with Srdjan Spasojevic on the extended cut of A Serbian Film, and maybe something later on his next film. Working with Jason Koch on A Serbian Documentary that is leading into the new film I wrote, To Become Unholy, with Jason directing. Doing the film fest circuit for Solomon and picking up more gore films for Unearthed. It's going to be an exciting year for all of us here... hope you all dig it.

IT'S BLOODIER AT MIDNIGHT

Nick Cato

I think I was in the fourth or fifth grade, circa 1978, when I first heard someone talk about a midnight movie. A girl in my class came in one Monday with a T-shirt featuring the image of a pair of ruby red lips, and she was speaking with her friends about a film her older sister had seen the previous weekend… a film that only screened at midnight. Being a horror film fan even at this young age, I was intrigued. After finding out the film she discussed was more of a comedy/musical than a straight-out horror movie, I was still interested to know just why it played so late at night. I stood there jealous, wishing I was older so I could go investigate this film for myself. And hence, my journey into the midnight movie phenomenon began.

It wasn't until late 1982 that I first got to see The Rocky Horror Picture Show at a twin theater in my hometown of Staten Island, NY. I enjoyed it well enough and a year later, I snuck into Manhattan to see it at the famous 8th Street Playhouse, where the audience participation thing had reached levels no one could had ever anticipated. So, I had finally seen what all the fuss was about, and at the time, I was fascinated with everything about it.

The 8th Street provided a practical crash course in midnight movie going. But it was a book titled Midnight Movies by Stuart Samuels (1983, Collier Books) where I received my first academic (if you will) education on midnight movies and the subculture surrounding them. This is where I learned audience participation had began long before people started hurling com-

ments at Tim Curry, and that maniacal fans had been going to other films religiously week after week.

I had seen Night of the Living Dead (1968) on late night TV when I was about six years old, and it made me a life-long fan of the genre. But Samuels' book explained that the film had an amazing midnight cult

following, and it was then that something started to stir in the back of my brain.

The chapter on 1971's Harold and Maude also spoke to me, as it bore witness of film fans who had faithfully lined up to see it weekend after weekend, in some theaters for over three years. The same with 1970's El Topo, 1972's Pink Flamingos, and 1977's Eraserhead, to name what were arguably the more popular midnight offerings of the time.

Then one week in the Village Voice, which to this day has an impressive film review section, I spotted ads for midnight

screenings of The Slumber Party Massacre as well as Basket Case, both 1982 films I had seen on VHS, but now playing at the witching hour at NYC's Waverly Twin (which today is the home of the IFC Center). I went completely out of my mind, as it was difficult for me at that age to get out of my strict suburban home to head into the city at those late hours. The aforementioned time I had managed to go to the 8th Street Playhouse, I "slept at a friend's house," so trying to pull that one again so soon just wasn't happening. My old man wasn't that clueless.

The early 1980s were painful in that, while I did attend just about every horror film that was released during regular hours, going to see certain screenings at midnight in Manhattan wasn't to happen for me for several more years. In the meantime, I bought all the local papers every Friday afternoon and scanned them for both midnight and regular screenings, making sure to attend all I could and dreaming about the late-night showings in the city I wouldn't be able to attend. The 8th Street Playhouse, at this time, featured midnight shows every single night of the week, and for a few weeks even featured Herschell Gordon Lewis' The Gore Gore Girls on Tuesday nights. This film wasn't yet available on video, but despite my begging and pleading with my old man, there was no way I was getting out on a "school night" for a midnight movie. When I could, I rented VHS tapes of current midnight films (such as 1983's Liquid Sky, which had become somewhat of a hit on the NYC midnight circuit) and watched them at home at midnight. In all honesty, there was nothing special about doing this, other than trying to capture something that was nearly impossible to recreate without a

BIZARRE HUMAN SACRIFICES!
The most Violent Film Ever!

BANNED IN 31 COUNTRIES

THEY RAPED & MURDERED HIS SISTER WHILE HE WATCHED HELPLESSLY. NOW IT'S HIS TURN TO...

MAKE THEM DIE SLOWLY

theater full of like-minded fans.

From approximately 1985-1991, I attended many midnight films in both Manhattan and nearby New Jersey (these were also the years I was fortunate enough to enjoy Times Square screenings at the end of their heyday). My Rocky Horror fascination had run its course by the time I was a sophomore in high school, but I was fully enjoying other cult classics such as A Clockwork Orange and Fritz the Cat whenever they screened. One local theater on Staten Island, the Island Twin, featured Rocky Horror in Theater One and a different midnight film in Theater Two every weekend. It was there where I got to experience films such as Urgh! A Music War, Day of the Dead, Dawn of the Dead, The Exorcist, Creepshow, and Pink Floyd - The Wall surrounded by other fans who understood the joy of seeing a midnight movie at midnight. There was a certain feeling at the Island Twin, the 8th Street Playhouse, and a little-known theater in south Jersey called the Cinema Alley that only lovers of obscure, weird, and horror cinema could relate to. In a way, it was magic. It made the film more special. Being out late at night with dedicated fans was like belonging to a community who only came out when the "normal" people had long gone home.

While I wasn't one who continually

went to the same movie week after week (aside from my two-year stint as a member of a local Rocky Horror crew), I did spend a lot of weekends going to midnight films, and regardless of the feature (which was usually horror oriented), I met people there who, to this day, I've stayed in touch with.

Due to my marriage and the raising of two kids, my midnight movie life took a major backseat from late 1991-2006. On occasion during those years I'd attend a midnight movie, but something happened around 2006 (at least in the NYC area) that continues to grow to this day: a couple of dedicated theaters have committed themselves to consistent midnight movie programming. I remember reading the Village Voice one day in 2007 and spotting an ad for Dario Argento's latest film The Mother of Tears, which was being screened in Manhattan at the Landmark Sunshine at midnight. I attended with an old friend, and regardless of what one feels about the film, the experience of seeing an Argento film with a theater full of Italian horror film fans was second to none. It was a night that re-sparked my desire to get back into the theaters at the witching hour, my growing age be damned (and yes, as I approach 50, staying up for midnight movies is getting harder and harder, but it's almost always worth the extra effort). Since then, I have seen many classic (and newer cult titles) at the Sunshine, including Henry: Portrait of a Serial Killer, I Drink Your Blood, Gone with the Pope, The Room, All About Evil, Pink Flamingos, and Dr. Butcher, MD to name a few.

Across town at the IFC Center (once home to classics midnight screenings as the Waverly Twin), I've had the privilege of seeing midnight film print screenings of El Topo, The Holy Mountain, A Clockwork Orange, Eraserhead, and newer titles such as Antibirth and the second two Human Centipede films (it should be noted that in 2011, at the NYC midnight premiere of The Human Centipede 2: Full Sequence, not only did the film sell out two theaters at the same time, but the theater I was in

NATIONAL PEEP EXTRA

"All the Print That's Fit to News"

IS THIS 'WOMAN' THE FILTHIEST PERSON ALIVE?

 Tarred, Feathered and Shot in Wierdo Feud

 Sex Change Operation Paid For by Welfare

had one of the liveliest crowds I had ever seen a film with. The enthusiasm that night was incredible, which made it all the more head-scratching that there were only eight of us in attendance when Part 3 screened in the same theater a few years later.).

Due in large part to the Nighthawk Cinema in Brooklyn (which opened in 2010), I have attended countless classic '70s and '80s horror films on their big screen at

YOU DON'T HAVE TO GO TO TEXAS FOR A CHAINSAW MASSACRE!

ABSOLUTELY NO ONE UNDER 17 ADMITTED TO THIS PERFORMANCE

PIECES

IT'S EXACTLY WHAT YOU THINK IT IS!

the midnight hour. Seeing Pieces (1982) the night it opened was fun, but seeing it again a few years ago with a theater full of hardcore fans was indescribable. Like classic midnight movie audiences of old, lines were repeated, some people spoke back to the screen, and everyone applauded and cheered when Lynda Day George's infamous overacting sequence ("Bastard! Bastard! BASTARD!") unreeled. Same for Lady Terminator (1989), which was the last film I got to see on 42nd Street before it became sanitized. Revisiting it at midnight with like-minded lunatics was as wonderful as you'd think. I had similar experiences there at recent late-night screenings of Cannibal Ferox, Fascination, Switchblade Sisters, Blood Feast, and Chopping Mall. Oh yeah… I even finally got to attend The Slumber Party Massacre with a proper midnight crowd.

From what I've heard from midnight movie fans around the country, it seems parts of Texas and Los Angeles have also been offering midnight goodies lately, and I often get hate mail on social media telling me to shut my trap about all the great midnight screenings I get to attend (hey, don't blame me for where you live!). I'm

lucky to live where I do, close to several theaters that feature new and classic horror and cult films every weekend when the sun goes down. I'm lucky to have this "bizarre subculture," as Stuart Samuels called it, so close to my backyard. And while I can't completely describe just what it is, there is something special about seeing an unusual film at midnight. Watching The Holy Mountain on Blu-ray is fine, but seeing it on the big screen is like witnessing a surreal painting come to life. Eraserhead is even easier to digest when you're in the middle of a packed theater of die-hard Lynchians. And Dawn of the Dead, Pieces, and Cannibal Ferox seem bloodier when they screen at the witching hour. I kid you not.

It seems only natural that horror films have a different feel when screened at midnight. While I've seen Stanley Kubrick's The Shining many times, it wasn't until 2016 that I attended a midnight screening. While sitting there with a sold-out theater of dedicated fans, something about the film felt even more unearthly than I had experienced before. There was a communal thing going on, despite being with mostly strangers. At this screening, we were all connected. We

weren't just at a movie theater but inside the Overlook itself. Any good film will suck the viewer into it, but being among hardcore fans at midnight screenings works

a kind of magic that the filmmakers themselves could never explain.

Maybe next time we'll talk about the 1990 NYC midnight premiere of Frankenhooker, where a stray cat under the screen provided as much entertainment as the film.

Now go get some sleep.

GORE SCOREBOARD

THE RATING SYSTEM

🐕 **bow-wow**

💀 **nearly worthless**

💀💀 **ordinary**

💀💀💀 **solid & scary**

💀💀💀💀 **hardcore horror**

THE GORE SCORE

This evaluation deals with nothing but the quantity of blood, brains, guts, and assorted precious bodily fluids spilled during the course of the film. It's quite simple, really. The Bad News Bears Go to Japan would get a big, fat zero in the Gore Score category, while Dr. Butcher, M.D. and Maniac would most likely receive juicy nines or tens.

0 — Mary Poppins, Dumbo, and Terms of Endearment

10 — Blood Sucking Freaks, The Evil Dead, and The Gates of Hell

—Chas Balun

(DZ) David Zuzelo; (DD) Dennis Daniel; (BH) Bruce Holecheck; (AE) Art Ettinger

---

THE TRANSFIGURATION (2017)

d: Michael O'Shea

💀💀💀💀 **7**

Every now and then, a genre film comes out that inexplicably falls off of virtually everyone's radar. I want to travel the world like a missionary, shouting from rooftops to spread the word about The Transfiguration. It tells the story of an extremely fucked-up urban teenager named Milo, who is obsessed with vampires to the point that fantasy and reality begin to merge. He's the kind of kid who thinks that a perfect date includes showing his favorite clips from Faces of Death to his potential love interest. A fresh take on themes explored in Martin, The Transfiguration is clever, cerebral, gory, wild, and completely batshit insane. It played festivals in 2016 before finally getting a theatrical release in 2017. Even well-watched, jaded viewers won't know where it's going. It's one of the grittiest coming-of-age horror stories of all time, and it blew my fucking mind. See it today! (AE)

PREVENGE (2016)

d: Alice Lowe

💀💀 **4**

"People think babies are sweet. But I'm bitter." Preggo Ruth is ready to pop, and, even worse, she's host to an articulate, judgmental, particularly bitchy fetus. Receiving telepathic direction from her parasitic tummy terror, she's spurred to slice down those deemed responsible for the father's untimely demise in a vague climbing accident. All between her regularly scheduled obstetrician appointments, of course. Ostensibly a horror comedy satirizing the stresses of pregnancy, Prevenge fails to really commit to either genre, rendering the film a somewhat unsatisfying watch as it drifts through its one-note scenario. There's an occasional laugh, but the murders lack any real energy or creativity—though it's admittedly hard not to perk up a little when slumming DJ Disco Dan is relieved of a gonad on his Grandmom's carpet. Alain Robak's Baby Blood (1990) did it all decades earlier, much better and much bloodier. (BH)

VIOLENT SHIT: THE MOVIE (2015)

d: Luigi Pastore

 8

Karl the Butcher is back, and has somehow found his way to Italy, home of the Pastapocalypse! But as soon as Karl is introduced, he vanishes amidst the proceedings, and a few quick killings inspire a ton of chatter that quickly gets boring. And, this my dear Reddites… this is not good. There is a sinister dude trying to harness the power of Shit (played by Cannibal Ferox Survivor Sweepstakes non-winner John Morghen) to liven things up, but he devours more scenery than Karl can kill.

The film looks great and sounds even better (Goblin maestro Claudio Simonetti provides a score that you'll be able to hum instantly if you've heard any of his work in the last 20 years), but, sad to say, things also get boring fast. Even the orgiastic wetness of the finale can't save it.

Reviving the Violent Shit series probably seemed like a good idea. But transporting things to Italy and leaving gorelord Andreas Schnaas out (barring said cameo) makes for an epic chatfest that reduces the impact of the overall feature to comedy. The decision to reduce splatter in favor of characterization—only to drag Italian icons like Enzo Castellari and Luigi Cozzi in to mug for the camera—is spinebreaking. These guys are champions of cinema, but their unfunny blather belongs in the outtakes. The ultimate insanity is making Karl the Butcher an afterthought in his own film. Schnaas brought a twisted vileness to his work. Here, his video sins are completely abandoned. Producer Steve Aquilina douched out the asshole of the horrors that begat the original icon of German video bodysmashing and mimicked the splatter hits from shits past.

There is gore. Damned good gore, at that. But when I think back and realize that the original movie (shot on video, with no real motive in mind beyond showcasing violence) was better paced, it makes me feel a twinge of sadness—even more so than the bizarre "comedic styling" of Violent Shit 4 did.

Sold in a stunning ultimate edition with extras (a CD soundtrack is also included), this is like sitting down to gobble up some German gore sausage… only to find the sad remnants of a turd shaped meatball on your plate. Don't be fooled by the Gore Score. It ALL happens at the end… far too late to save this Violent Shit from taking a dump on your day. (DZ)

THE HONEYMOON KILLERS (1969)

d: Leonard Kastle

  2

Movies based on true stories can never really be anything but fiction. They take artifice to make things seem true and put you into their own world of truth. The Honeymoon Killers does this in such an unsettling way that you tend to lose yourself in the world that it artfully projects… even if what you're seeing is a pastiche of the truth. And as far as pastiches go, THK makes a great case for bringing as much truth as possible into a movie.

For a one-shot film from first-time director and screenwriter Leonard Kastle, the film packs quite a wallop. The use of Gustav Mahler's 5th and 6th symphonies gives the thing a surreal and eerie quality.

From the moment the movies starts, you feel like a fly on the wall watching reality in black and white. The camera is lucid, and sways in and out of faces, bodies and rooms… as if you WERE a fly! You plunge into the story of Martha Beck (played with incredible pathos and blank-eyed cruelty by the late, great Shirley Stoler), a fat, unhappy bitch of a nurse who rules her roost with a pudgy hand and wants no shenanigans going on in any back rooms! If she can't have fun, no one can! She's in that horrible state of limbo where life consists of going to work, returning home, and eating lots of pretzels and candy in order to drown away those "I'm too ugly" blues.

When her friend Bunny (an annoying as ever Doris Roberts) gets her to join a lonely-hearts club, she falls head over heels with Raymond Fernandez (played with suitable charm and bile by Tony Lo Bianco), a scheming, greasy low-life hustler who charms old ladies and sad middle-aged women into giving him all their money—which he absconds with post haste! But in the case of Martha, something clicks. When he comes to seduce her, you can sense the attraction. "Don't be a shy nurse," he says, as he sambas over to a fade out. You can feel the connection in the letters they write, presented with narration from the principles. For whatever reason, this unlikely duo goes together like two rats in a sewer! When Martha finds out about his devious con-man ways, it matters none! Raymond is a crook? Oh, well. She loves him so much that she wants to play along! So, she dumps her mom in an old folks home and hops on the lonely-hearts bandwagon of deception. In each duping scenario, she plays his sister. Only trouble is, she has a raging jealousy and insecurity that threatens the very fabric of their cause! As soon as any of the female-fodder romantics start to get cushy with Raymond, Martha goes beserko! In one case, she gives an overdose of pills to a pregnant victim (Marilyn Chris), who is put on a bus and left to die.

They try to find some domestic tranquility in Valley Stream, Long Island… living in a little house on a little street in a little town. HA! NO GOOD! Raymond craves the game and the money! And the game will, from now on, lead to murder. Horrendous murder.

This is when the film gets really ugly and profoundly disturbing. When you consider that it was made in 1969, a shaky time in history, as well as a time when all kinds of new taboos were being broken in the burgeoning independent cinema universe (and in major studio productions, as well), it still is rather off-putting to see the cold reality of how these murders took place. Director Leonard Kastle gives them to you both graphically and suggestively. The murder of Janet Fay (Mary Jane Higby) is especially gruesome, all the more so because her character is such an innocent. She is bludgeoned by a hammer and strangled... up close and personal. The documentary style only adds to the revulsion. It happens almost by accident, but once it's done, the sense of remorse is quickly overshadowed by the work of getting rid of the evidence. Two more murders take place. You look on in horror as the two characters slowly lose all sense of reality. Martha is the one who eventually cracks, because Raymond has NEVER kept his promise of not sleeping with any of the victims. After the last two murders, she calls the police, unbeknownst to Raymond. The film ends with Martha reading a letter from Raymond, who still loves her despite their situation.

I've been a true crime fan since I was a teenager, and the "Lonely Hearts Murders" are a staple of every book about the history of homicide. It really is a fascinating, sick story. A story that the film follows (albeit with many changes) and portrays almost TOO faithfully. (DD)

BERLIN SYNDROME (2017)

d: Cate Shortland

Young, cute Clare boxes up her life in Australia for a backpacking jaunt through Europe, in search of those "life experiences" she's heard so much about. Spending a few days in a German hostel, paths cross with Andi, a charismatic schoolteacher with whom Clare feels an instant connection. Postponing plans to head for Dresden, things get hot and sweaty that night, but when Andi leaves for work the next morning, she finds herself locked in his remote apartment. The key he left doesn't work. The SIM card is missing from her phone. The windows are made of reinforced glass. There are no neighbors to help. Even worse, she finds clues indicating she may not be the first.

A well-made abduction thriller chronicling Clare's ongoing acceptance and adapting of her new living situation, Berlin Syndrome primarily works because of the dedicated, nuanced performances from its two leads. It's a grim subject, handled realistically, but its dramatic aspirations somewhat

mute anything truly daring—even at its most tense, there aren't any real surprises. In the end, it's still essentially just a glorified Lifetime movie, with more nipples and less John Stamos. (BH)

JUDAS GHOST (2013)

d: Simon Pearce

I can only imagine the phrases that Chas Balun would have used if he was confronted by the endless loop of found footage/shaky cam non-epics that beat a horror fanatic's digital doorway down via endless streaming services and clever titles hiding dog dick biting pseudofilms (where nothing happens... at all). Judas Ghost starts with a splat and introduces a mercifully underused "streaming" element that had me shaking in my monster PJ pants at the thought of another night of cinematic pablum. But, before a stream of fear-induced piss could be loosed, things took a turn.

Written by popular spooky horror scribe Simon R. Green, we are dropped headlong into his "Ghost Finders" universe of novels. A squad of ghost smashers with supernatural knowledge and psychic abilities (yawn) enters a haunted hall for kiddie care (groan) and sets up a camera (gag). The supernatural shit goes down as doors appear and disappear... and much pseudoscience from the Carnacki Institute is slung with abandon. Scenery gets chomped, evil things encroach, and it's an ectoplasmically intense ride from there.

Against a shallow backdrop of potential clichés, Simon R. Green's script blends well with Simon Pearce's knack for making one room visually viable for less than an 80-minute runtime. This works far better than 99% of the shaky-cam soap operas that pass for paranormal thrillers. Using an obviously minuscule budget, Judas Ghost was meant to be a proving ground for Green's concepts, and this damned bit of potential cinematic ennui passes the "did not doze off watching a security cam" test with ease. Instead of Paranormal Activity, we get something like an early Dr. Who with swearing... and a pile of body parts drenched in gothblack blood. The main cast of five exorcise their roles into a smattering of slime from beyond, and the technicians behind the camera create a genuine sense of dread that doesn't lose itself amidst the spartan splatter. Check out the books and watch the flicks. Welcome to the Carnacki Institute clan. "We don't take any shit from the Hereafter!" (DZ)

LEATHERFACE (2017)

d: Julien Maury and Alexandre Bustillo

1955. After dropping an engine block on the sheriff's daughter, the youngest Sawyer boy (and future skin-stealer) Jed is sent away to the Gorman House Youth Reformatory—a thinly-veiled insane asylum whose children are routinely juiced in the name of therapy. A decade later, Mom Sawyer thinks she has the proper paperwork for a family reunion, but instead instigates a full-on riot, during which a pair of thrill-kill lovers escape with her son, a kidnapped nurse, and another inmate. From there, it's murder on the open road, as the sexed-up psychopaths plan to break across the border, but Sheriff Daughterless is still holding a mean grudge and won't stop until that darn Sawyer kid's in the ground where he belongs…

The biggest hurdle an origin story has to overcome is its own unnecessary existence. One of the most unsettling aspects of Hooper's original The Texas Chain Saw Massacre (1974) was its lack of explanation—its family simply existed, there in the heat, waiting for their next victims. Does Leatherface manage to overcome the odds and successfully prove itself a worthy prequel? Fuck no. Not even close. Even divorced from its franchise heritage it's not particularly great, but if you're feeling especially forgiving, it's passable-enough Texas splat (filmed in Bulgaria, for maximum verisimilitude) that's thankfully a little more trashy and mean-spirited than the last few installments. Spurting neck wounds. Face blown off. Face reattached. Pigsty smorgasbord. Chainsawed digits. Chainsawed torso. Chainsaw decapitation. Abandoned trailer necro-sex. One very unusual hiding spot. Somehow Stephen Dorff and Lili Taylor are in this thing. You've spent worse 88 minutes. (BH)

SLASHER.COM (2017)

d: Chip Gubera

The US DVD cover promises that 2017's Slasher.com is a Tinder for terror seekers, but what gorehounds hungry for hookups ultimately get is a clever riff on the "who's stalking who?" genre that's off-kilter enough to overcome such self-aware shit like a "MYERS RENTALS" sign (posted in paint) on a cheap cabin in the woods. Still, the familiar porn/low budget horror trick of heavy lifting by genre vets (with the help from some awkward first timers) works in a true gonzo fashion. And while it takes a while for things to get going, the antics of the final 30 minutes provide a good payoff pop. After a dull opening murder scene sets the stage for boredom, a duo on a date (set up via the internet, natch) decide to head on out for a weekend rendezvous.

Kristy and Jack are quite the couple. Both suspicious in their nerdiness, their mega-sexed banter is enough to make you wonder if there really is something going on, or if they were just scooped off the set of a terrible softcore film. They flirt. They fuck. And then, the trap is sprung… and your fears of wasting a few bucks on the film subside just long enough for it to wrap up its sub-90-minute runtime.

Slasher.com gets points for introducing Momma (Jewel Shepard) and Jesse (my second favorite Leatherface, R.A. Mihailoff). And, let's not forget their goofy hot daughter (daddy has an affinity for her that goes far beyond the sawing that you'd expect from R.A.). The two gore vets devour more screen than Deodato's cannibals ever dreamed! They torment their visitors with pain wrought by flesh, rage and… spoon?

Yep! Jewel Shepard dials up a performance for the ages as her character spoons out her own crotch and slurps from freshly self-shat corpses! If there was a Gag Score, this bit would go for the gusto with a 10! There are double crosses, quadruple crosses, and gore scenes that are too far and few between (but still effective enough to merit your time). But really—come for the slashing, and stay for Jewel Shepard. With boobs, facial impaling, and a goofy finale that actually works, Slasher.com is one of those films you'll find in 20 packs soon enough. Dig in! SLURP…*CHOKE* (DZ)

THE GIRL WITH ALL THE GIFTS (2016)

d: Colm McCarthy

"The girl in my story didn't eat people!" Meet Melanie. A precocious, inquisitive kid. Proper student. Loves Velcro. Never lies. Occasionally eats worms and cats. Ten years after a fungal infection turned the majority of Earth's population into zomboid "Hungries," a group of military scientists remain optimistic. They believe a class of children, contaminated in utero, may hold the key, but when their compound falls to the ever-growing hordes of flesh-crazed invaders, their new priority becomes saving Melanie, as she may be humanity's last hope for a cure.

Adapted from a popular book with a name cast and decent budget, The Girl with all the Gifts gets credit for breathing some life back into a subgenre that's inarguably been beating an undead horse for the last decade. Newcomer Sennia Nanua shines as the naïve, wide-eyed Melanie, eliciting sympathy but still maintaining a feral edge—her sweet, childlike demeanor fools just enough, but you never quite forget she's capable of biting your face off. Despite a few convenient missteps that seemingly exist only to put characters in jeopardy, the film still manages a few surprises, and overall remains a winner worth checking out. Besides, it's probably the only chance you'll ever have to see Glenn Close brain someone with a fire extinguisher. (BH)

NECRONOS-TOWER OF DOOM (2011)

d: Marc Rohnstock

German gore! It brings splatterhounds together and slaughters the eyeballs of anyone looking for narrative and conventional filmmaking! Marc Rohnstock and his Infernal Films bring Necronos to raging life in a two-hour gore epic that pushes the Gore Score to its maximum with sledgehammer sluggings, brutal impalings, and the revelation that you can somehow make a two-hour movie with full female nudity without showing a medieval bit of bush. There ain't a pubic hair to be found amidst the chaos!

But we don't come the land of Teutonic Terror for pubic foliage. We come for the sensory overload of cheap shocks. And Necronos brings plenty.

Necronos is a wizard who meets his demented demise in a distant time, but Satan isn't content to let him go. With a little bit of time leaping, the mad mystic and his grotesque servant Goran are out to (get this!) find THE CHOSEN ONE... and she had better be a virgin! But that isn't enough, because they need a lot of meat to mash up—Necronos is also building himself a skin-shredding berserker! To top things off, he also has to deal with a crazy witch played by the familiar German splatter actress Manoush! That's a lot of cinematic tropes to squish into a small, fleshy bag of a film, but things never get boring. In fact, the overlong running time flows along as quickly as the blood that squirts out of the impaled victims of Goran and his gruesome grinders!

Loaded with enough practical gore effects to satisfy those disgusted by CGI, Rohnstock and his crew are fearless in executing monster suits, flying limbs, and more shredded latex than you'd find at a one-off sale on irregular Ron Jeremy replica dildos. It's easy to get caught up in the trashy excellence of the technical execution. While hardly a film that will leave you thinking about what happened in its overcomplicated plot, Necronos-Tower of Doom is a living, screaming, grindcore album cover come to cinematic life! (DZ)

KILLER RACK (2015)

d: Greg Lamberson

Director Greg Lamberson (Slime City) unhooks and unleashes his best film to date with a tale that answers the question, "When TITillation becomes terror... who will survive the onslaught of these ferocious funbags?" You will—and you'll laugh, gawk, and shock your way through Killer Rack like the first time you found a copy of Juggs on the train tracks! Stitching together a gross-out comedy (complete with a musical number!), Lamberson tells the tale of a flat-chested

sweetheart named Betty Downer, who is so sick with bazonga-envy that she will go to any length to increase her mammorial splendor. She finds her way to the blood-drenched door of Dr. Cate Thulu, whose plan to implant the Whoppers of War into her tiny frame causes havoc all around. She gets passed over for a job at work? ENTER THE BREASTS, and it's promotion time! Boyfriend not attentive enough? SHOW HIM TITS!

As the world opens up to Betty, it is also coming apart. A dark force sends her into the world to devour and demolish ALL FLESH! Heckle this frame, and you'll go insane before losing your brain on the street. Will Betty find love? Will Lloyd Kaufman grate on our nerves with another cameo? All of this is answered with BOSOMY results that will keep you slurpin' from the terror-teats.

Your reviewer is a hater of horror comedy, but this servant of Slime Cinema was amazed that most of the jokes work and benefit buxotically from the performances of veteran titans of scream cinema, including Debbie Rochon (Chainsaw Cheerleaders) and Michael Thurber (Seven Dorms of Death). The film's knockers rest firmly in the cups of Jessica Zwolak (Johnny Gruesome), who keeps her center of balance as the gravitational pull of the massive killer rack is strapped to her already perky talents. The effects are wet, and splatterhounds will be tickled to see Roy (Street Trash) Frumkes show up for a flesh-ripping meltdown! The DVD is bursting-at-the-brastraps with extras, and should certainly motorboat its way into your collection of titty terrors! (DZ)

DERANGED (1974)

d: Jeff Gillen, Alan Ormsby

Deranged! On Blu-ray! OK... this is a thing of beauty! I can remember not too long ago when the only way I could see Deranged was on a fifth-generation dupe that Steve Bissette lent me in the late '80s! I remember reading about the film in The Psychotronic Film Guide. I even thought that the poster shot of Roberts Blossom (as Ezra Cobb) made him look exactly like Ed Gein. This movie was legendary back in the horror boom of the '80s! Why, even Tom Savini was involved! Who'd a-thunk it?

Alas... it was a drive-in movie that came and went long ago. A must-see that was almost impossible to be seen.

Now here I am watching it in all of its Blu-ray crystalline glory! Released by Kino Lorber, no less! Class-eeeeee!

Oh yes, Deranged is worth the time of any horror fan. The best attempt ever to tell the story of Ed Gein. Produced by Alan "Children Shouldn't Play with Dead Things" Ormsby and Bob "A Christmas Story" Clark, this is one eerie, disturbing gem of a horror film. All the more horrific because it's so close to the real-life story! Well, I mean... as close as any that had been made at that time.

The documentary style is very nerve-jangling because it's done in such a serious tone. The narrator/newsman character (Les Carlson of Videodrome fame) interjects himself within scenes so that the camera holds both the narrator and characters within the same frame. The organ music (which always shows up at just the right moment) is depressing, minimalist, and dour. It perfectly creates an unsettling mood. The acting is top-notch for a film of this nature and budget! Cosette Lee (as Ezra's mother) gives off the perfect sense of a bible-thumping, woman hating, fanatical Christian. Her warnings to Ezra about women are so off-putting that they'll make ya think twice! (Just kidding.) The supporting cast is clueless-country-bumpkin-enough to be believable. And then, of course, there's Roberts Blossom. His performance alone is worth the price of admission. Look at that blank, bewildered face! Those wild eyes! That quivering bottom lip. The way he shoves pea soup into his dying mother's mouth—"It's good and hot!" He truly embodies the sad sack mamma's boy reality of what Gein was most likely like! His slow and steady decline into madness is handled with kid gloves by directors Ormsby and Gillen. True, he does look crazy from the get-go (it is Roberts Blossom, after all)... but where he gets going is even more crazyland! Things do get quite scary... and downright perverted by the end.

If you've seen the film before, you know its qualities. If you've never seen it, then stop what you're doing and order the Blu-ray this instant! No card-carrying horror film fan should be without a copy of Deranged! A pristine copy, I might add!

Deranged belongs right beside The Texas Chain Saw Massacre as a fitting cinematic tribute to the depravity of one Ed Gein. They don't make them like this anymore. The time for this kind of production has long since vanished. That's what makes Deranged all the more special. Something that was once impossible to see is now presented in a way that speaks to its importance in the canon of great horror films.

And Deranged is a GREAT horror film... make no mistake about that! (DD)

PSYCHO COP RETURNS (1993) ⑥

d: Adam Rifkin

💀 💀 💀 💀

Director Adam Rifkin (The Dark Backward) will tell you that he never bothered to watch Psycho Cop, and you won't need to either, although the experience does have merits of its own. Psycho Cop Returns is an insanely fun ride that twists the tried and true exploitation tropes of bachelor parties and psychotic police into a billy-clubbing beatdown of any viewer lucky enough to get forgetful and not pass the donuts to the local lawman.

When a group of ne'er do wells decides to throw a stag night for a bud at work (overseen by Bill Paxton's DAD, who gets to mutter "asshole" with vigor), the boobs and hired tits run afoul of Officer Joe Vickers. This cop packs a patrol car full of body parts (!), and wisecracks about mass mutilation whenever inappropriate. After some prime gonzola booty dancing (including a sequence with Julie "The Amazon Prime" Strain), the law goes to work and starts annihilating everyone in sight. Popped out eyeballs and a double-nude-pentagram-kebab are just some of the highlights. From the first goofy frame to the final scene, this is a great little stalk 'n' slash number with boobs, bullets, and blood galore that never loses sight of the fun of a baddie that just says BOO!

Written by Dan Povenmire of The Simpsons and Phineas and Ferb fame, the whole thing is an entertaining work that keeps things bloody and packs in more laughs than all of the Sorority House Massacres combined. Rifkin makes the redressed hallway chases entertaining as Bobby Ray Vickers (Robert R. Shafer of The Office) delivers, "You have the right to remain DEAD!" with more gusto than a horde of scream queens saying EEEEEEK! Big bonus points for Povennmire's band Keep Left and their track "Talkin' 'bout Aaargh" for a slasher theme for the eons.

The Vinegar Syndrome release contains the uncensored director's cut, documentaries, a commentary track, and everything you need to feel the total beatdown of the Psycho Cop! (DZ)

DEEP RED™ WILL RETURN.